OLD FRONTENAC Minnesota

Its History and Architecture

KEN ALLSEN

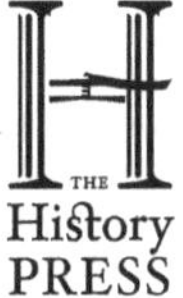

Published by The History Press
Charleston, SC 29403
www.historypress.net

Images are from the author's collection unless otherwise noted.

First published 2011
Second printing 2013

Manufactured in the United States

ISBN 978.1.59629.507.0

Library of Congress Cataloging-in-Publication Data

Allsen, Ken.
Old Frontenac, Minnesota : its history and architecture / Ken Allsen.
p. cm.
Includes bibliographical references.
ISBN 978-1-59629-507-0
1. Old Frontenac (Minn.)--History. 2. Historic buildings--Minnesota--Old Frontenac. 3. Architecture--Minnesota--Old Frontenac. 4. Old Frontenac (Minn.)--Buildings, structures, etc. I. Title.
F614.O38A45 2011
977.6'14--dc22
2010050609

This book is dedicated to the residents of Frontenac—
past, present and future.

Then Frontenac looms upon our vision, delightful resort of jaded summer tourists.

—Mark Twain, Life on the Mississippi, *1871*

I fell in love with this place forty years ago, and I have been in love with it ever since.

—Israel Garrard, 1895

Contents

Preface

Shortly after moving to Rochester, Minnesota, in 1966, I discovered Lake Pepin on the Mississippi River, thirty-five miles to the north, and soon started spending time sailing on its waters and exploring its banks by automobile. An early discovery was a small village fronting the lake with a number of large houses obviously dating from the middle of the nineteenth century. Where we lived before, in the mid–Hudson Valley in New York, buildings from the nineteenth century were fairly common, and buildings like these in Frontenac did not warrant much attention, unless they were once occupied by someone really notable. But in Minnesota, they are not common, especially such a large number of structures still extant in an original pastoral setting.

I immediately set out to read whatever I could find on the history of the buildings and found that no really detailed analysis existed. Busy with career and family, I did not even conceive of undertaking the project myself. But over the years, I returned to Frontenac many times, exploring and gathering what material I could. After my retirement from a long career at IBM in 1995, I finally was able to fully dedicate myself to architectural history. I discovered that I loved to research buildings and write about them. Among other things, this led to my organizing and leading architectural walking tours. One of these tours was of Frontenac, a few years ago, for our state chapter of the Society of Architectural Historians. Ever growing in the back of my mind was an urge to document the buildings of this little time capsule on the Mississippi River. After publication of two books on the architecture of Rochester, Minnesota, my hometown, I finally felt ready for the task. Late in 2009, I began renewing old contacts in Frontenac and making new ones, surveying the availability of material for the project. The response was favorable, and this project was born.

Preface

Experience has taught me that writing about structures is meaningless unless an effort is made first to establish a context for their existence. Only when one knows why a building was erected on a particular site, at a particular time, by a particular person can the structure truly be brought to life. Part I of this book is dedicated to the history of the land and the people who used it, culminating in this small enclave of buildings. Its history is incredibly rich. It starts with the geological anomaly of Lake Pepin, part of that great river that has been a route of conquest and commerce for centuries. An understanding of the people who used the land and the river—Native Americans, French traders and American settlers—is also necessary to establish a context for the buildings described in Part II. There are a number of very nice homes in and around Frontenac, but I have restricted this effort to include only those built before 1900.

The scarcity of primary source materials made this project particularly challenging. A handful of original letters is available, and the original property records exist in abstracts and tax records. No copies of plans exist for the buildings, and most of them were probably built without benefit of formal drawings in the first place. Much of the known history of Frontenac is anecdotal, preserved by local residents. My task was to gather as much of this material as I could and verify it by cross-checking against written records wherever possible. The mainline text reflects the verified facts to the best of my ability. Local lore in many cases tells interesting stories, and these are preserved in the endnotes wherever they contribute to the history of the buildings. The images in this book are mostly archival and are donated by current residents who share a love for this place and wish to see it documented for posterity.

Having been fortunate enough to travel widely in my life, I have many favorite places to which I have returned or hope to return one day. One of these just happens to be in my own backyard. I hope you enjoy this literary tour of Old Frontenac and find as much pleasure in reading it as I did in creating it.

Acknowledgements

Many people gave me input on this project and shared materials with me. Bill Webster and Bill Flies, both residents of Frontenac, generously provided images from their own collections and shared their extensive knowledge with me. Other Frontenac homeowners were also kind enough to let me tour their properties and take photographs, and they shared a great deal of anecdotal material with me. Joyce Engstrom and Judy Johnson of the Friends of Florence Town Hall gave me free run of their extensive Frontenac archives at the town hall. I also thank the staffs at the Public Libraries of Red Wing and Lake City, the Goodhue and Wabasha County Historical Societies and the Minnesota Historical Society for their assistance.

And, as usual, I must express my love and gratitude to Nancy, my wife of more than fifty years. A partner in all these little literary efforts, she serves as first reader, grammarian, booster and an anchor when I go off course.

Part I

A History of Frontenac

The Land (Before 1853)

As the Mississippi River makes its way southward from its source in Minnesota's Lake Itasca to the Gulf of Mexico, it adopts the waters of many rivers, great and small. As it proceeds, it widens from a mere trickle at its source to the mighty waterway that has always been a highway of both conquest and trade. At the site of the current city of St. Paul, the first two rivers of significant size join the still modest Mississippi. From its union with the Minnesota and the St. Croix, a newly strengthened river courses southward. At a point about one hundred miles downstream, the Chippewa River enters the Mississippi from the Wisconsin side. For many ages, this river has forced its load of sand across the stream, building up bars to form a natural barrier to the big river. This has caused the creation of one of the most unique natural formations on the river, Lake Pepin. From its foot near the town of Reads Landing to its head just south of Red Wing, the lake stretches for almost thirty miles. At its widest point, it is nearly three miles across. Its banks are flanked by wooded bluffs four hundred feet in height. In many places, these bluffs are placed with their feet almost touching the river, but at others, the bluffs recede inland to reveal large tracts of fertile bottomland. It was in these areas that the current towns along the lakeshore would come into existence.

At its head, the lake runs in a due easterly course for about nine miles. It then makes a sweeping turn southeastward and proceeds past Lake City about six miles below. As the lake makes this turn, the bluffs that tower over it give the appearance to travelers on the water of a large point of land, though that is merely an optical illusion. Thus, this feature has come to be called "Point No Point." About a mile below, a true point does jut out into the lake. Named Pont au Sable (Sand Point) by early French traders,[1] it would be the site of the first white settlement on the western shore of Lake Pepin. On modern maps, this point is now called Long Point. Upstream from Long Point, another much smaller point extends into the lake, now called Frontenac Point. Between these two points was a narrow strip of gravelly beach, affording easy access to the land beyond. The land along this beach area was very low and subject to seasonal flooding, but just inland it rose extensively, forming a flat plain that ran westward to the bluffs more than two miles away. This area was crisscrossed by a system of ponds formed by a small creek that arose in the bluffs and finally entered the lake near Long Point. This, then, was the setting for our story, the saga of a small village named Frontenac.

Before white settlement in the area, this was the domain of the tribe named Sioux by the French but called Dakota in its own language.[2] Forced westward across the Mississippi by hostile tribes many years[3] before white explorers first encountered them, these hardy people spread westward across the current state of Minnesota into the wide-open lands beyond, as far as current South Dakota. Adopting the horse-based culture of the plains, these nomads were equally at home in the savannahs and hardwood forests of southeastern Minnesota, where game was plentiful and bottomland was available for primitive cultivation. Constrained on three sides, this group quickly learned the importance of defending its territory. To the north, the Chippewa (Ojibwe) held sway over the land around Lake Superior and were the first to make continuous trading contacts with the French. Armed with trade muskets, they moved ever southward, pressing for more territory to control in their pursuit of furs for trade. This brought them into constant conflict with the Dakota, who, in spite of their lack of firearms, managed to hold the line in a number of vicious battles that stretched over many years.

Across the Mississippi on the Wisconsin shore was another set of longtime foes, the Fox tribe and its allies, the Kickapoo. These were among the tribes that had originally forced the Dakota across the river, and their mutual enmity ran deep. As trade eventually increased with whites, competition between the warlike Fox and the equally bellicose Dakota often erupted into bloodshed and murder. And finally, from the south and up the river, came the final threat to the Dakota way of life. As white traders were followed inevitably by white settlers and white laws, the vise would tighten.

By the late seventeenth century, the French had a strong presence in North America. From their primary base in Quebec, they made their way down the St. Lawrence into the Great Lakes and the lands beyond. Initially, they came to trade, mapping new territory as they went. Accompanying them were the Jesuit priests of the Roman Catholic Church who had their own mission—

that of bringing Christianity to the native peoples wherever they could. Initially, these French parties made their way to the upper Mississippi River by way of Green Bay on Lake Michigan. From there, the route ran through Lake Winnebago and up the Fox River to near the current city of Portage, Wisconsin. Here they made a short overland transit to the Wisconsin River and then downstream to its mouth on the Mississippi. At this junction, the French established a major fort and trading facility at Prairie du Chien. From this base, French parties moved in both directions, attracting native tribes to the river's banks to trade their furs and hides for what must have appeared to them to be miraculous items of great value. And with the traders came the Jesuits to add stories of yet another miracle that became gradually absorbed into their already well-established native system of belief.

In the late 1600s, as the French opened the route through Lake Superior and trade was established with the Ojibwe, the furs available along Lake Pepin became of secondary importance, though still worthy of exploitation. Posts were established along the eastern bank of the Mississippi from the base at Prairie du Chien as far north as Lake Pepin. Fort St. Antoine, located about two miles south of the present town of Stockholm, Wisconsin, was established in 1685 by Nicholas Perrot. An experienced trader and explorer, his intention was to establish trade with the Dakota on the west bank of the river while trying to maintain friendly relations with the Kickapoo and Fox of the east bank. Trade with the Dakota proved to be brisk, but constant bloody confrontations between the tribes taxed Perrot's diplomatic skills. After ten years of productive existence, Fort St. Antoine was finally abandoned when Louis XV ordered all western forts to be closed. In its final year of existence, Fort St. Antoine saw the passage of the last major push up the river by the French, a party led by Pierre Charles LeSueur. He would establish a temporary post at Prairie Island,[4] north of Red Wing, then enter the Minnesota River and go up as far as the current site of Mankato. By 1700, however, the entire upper Mississippi area had entered a quarter century of temporary limbo as a trading area. As European politics swirled and the English tried to fathom how they might gain control of this important artery of trade, Lake Pepin waited quietly.

In 1727, the French would finally return to the western shore of the lake. A number of parties were dispatched by the Marquis de Beauharnois, governor general of Canada, to resume French control of the upper river and to discourage English encroachment. One of these, led by the Sieur de Perriere and accompanied by two Jesuit priests, landed on Pont au Sable (now Long Point) and established the first permanent post on the west bank of Lake Pepin. Named for the governor general of Canada, Fort Beauharnois was erected on the sandy soil. A chapel was created in a small hut for use by the two priests to serve their obligatory masses. Named for Saint Michael the Archangel, it would be the first Christian church in Minnesota. In the spring of 1728, the post was inundated by seasonal flooding. This fort remained in existence until 1729, in constant peril from Fox warriors intent on plunder and murder, in addition to the threat of another flood. Then, finally despairing of their situation, the occupants withdrew and burned the fort.

The benefit of having a trading outlet was apparent to the native peoples in the area, so they petitioned to have it restored. In 1731, a party under the Sieur de Linctot returned and rebuilt the fort, this time on higher ground in a better defensive position and safe from flooding. This site was on the current property of Villa Maria. Tribal unrest caused another temporary withdrawal between 1737 and 1750. In that year, the fort was rebuilt, and it operated until the French and Indian War compounded the difficulty of maintaining it. In 1756, the occupants finally abandoned the post for good. Fort Beauharnois was the last French fort in the upper Mississippi Valley.

By 1800, the French influence had passed to Spain, which then laid claim to all lands west of the Mississippi. It called this vast territory "Louisiana," a name originally given by the French, but the Spanish colonial authorities in New Orleans never actively moved to develop their foothold in the upper reaches of the river. Napoleon Bonaparte gained total control of France in 1800 and, by sheer intimidation, convinced Spain to allow Louisiana to revert to France. Spain received only some minor French conquests in Italy in exchange for its large territory in North America. The United States had already extended its western borders to the banks of the Mississippi River via the Treaty of Paris in 1783.[5] By 1802, Napoleon realized the impossibility of balancing his many European conflicts with the defense and development of Louisiana and approached the United States with an offer. In 1803, the United States made the Louisiana Purchase. For the first time, both banks of Lake Pepin were American.

In 1805, a party of American soldiers under Zebulon Pike explored the upper Mississippi as far as Leech Lake, returning with detailed maps of the land known to the Native Americans as "Minnesota" showing the many tributaries that entered the river from the west. It was quickly agreed that a fort at the confluence of the Minnesota and Mississippi Rivers would best serve to control trade and stabilize the native tribes, plus prevent further traffic by French or English traders. The War of 1812 would delay the implementation of this decision. In 1819, Colonel Leavenworth finally arrived at the chosen site, where he laid out an impressive stone strongpoint high above the meeting place of the two rivers. Around this site would grow the current cities of Minneapolis and St. Paul. In 1820, Colonel Josiah Snelling assumed command, and the new fort eventually received his name.[6] One member of the troops that arrived a few years later to join the garrison of Fort Snelling was Private James Wells.

James C. Wells was born in New Jersey in 1804. He joined the army in 1824 at the age of twenty, already a large and powerful figure. This, combined with an aggressive nature, served him well in the army and earned from his fellow soldiers the nickname "Bully." He was assigned to duty at Fort Snelling shortly after his enlistment. Remaining stationed at the fort until about 1835, Wells then left the army. He set himself up as a trader, first with a post at Chaska and then another in Waseca County. During this period, he married his wife, Jane, a daughter of early trader Duncan Graham and Hazahatwin, daughter of a Dakota chief. In 1837, they arrived at the future site of Frontenac, where he set up the post that would be their home for the next sixteen years. Wells would be the first white American permanent settler in Goodhue County.

Early steamboats[7] plying the upper river came to know the trading post on the gravel beach above Long Point. It became known first by its Dakota name, Waconia,[8] and later as Western Landing. Two small stone buildings provided both living and trading accommodations for the Wells family, surrounded by a large or small number of Dakota lodges, depending on the season. Wells's familial connection with the Dakota through his wife, plus a reputation for fairness, ensured continued good relations. Wells would prosper at Waconia and would also participate in the early political history of Minnesota. In 1849, the Minnesota Territory was established by an act of Congress. Wells served in three territorial legislatures between 1849 and 1853, maintaining many contacts in the settlements growing up around Fort Snelling. Another pioneer trader, Alexander Faribault,[9] was married to Jane Wells's sister, Elizabeth. Like his brother-in-law, Faribault was active in early Minnesota politics and served with him in the territorial legislature.

In 1830, agents of the United States called a council at Prairie du Chien, inviting Dakota, Sac, Winnebago and Fox tribal representatives. The intent was to foster peace in the area, as the constant warfare among the native people was interfering with trading interests along the upper river. Chief Wabasha,[10] one of the Dakota representatives present at the council, was induced to surrender a large tract of Dakota territory on the western bank of Lake Pepin. This was stated as being for the use of mixed-blood Dakota, though most of the land involved would actually fall under the control of early traders who had taken Dakota women as wives. The treaty resulting from the council contained a clause that allowed the federal government to assign tracts of

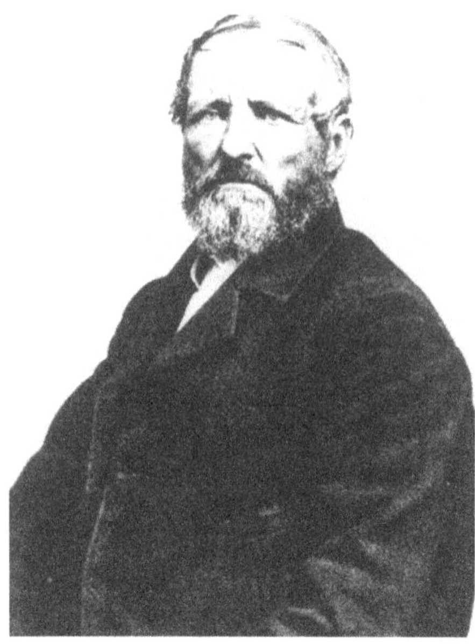

James C. "Bully" Wells, soldier, trapper, trader and politician. *Friends Collection.*

land of up to 640 acres to selected Dakota half-bloods. The area ultimately surveyed would contain approximately 320,000 acres, taken from tribal land allocated to the Dakota in previous treaties. The so-called "half-breed tracts" occupied a rectangle about fifteen by thirty-two miles in size with its long side facing Lake Pepin. At its upper end, the boundary extended from Barn Bluff in Red Wing in a southwesterly direction past the current town of Goodhue and then southeast well past the current town of Plainview to the banks of Beaver Creek. It then turned northeast, rejoining the river near the current town of Kellogg.

In 1851, the United States government entered into two further treaties with the Dakota. The first, signed at Traverse de Sioux on July 23, would ultimately confine the Dakota to a narrow strip along both banks of the Minnesota River, freeing up most of southern Minnesota for white settlement. Subsequent details were refined in a second treaty signed at Mendota on August 5. No special provision was made in these treaties for mixed-blood Dakota, many of whom still held rights to the land allocated to them two decades before on the shore of Lake Pepin. Through no fault of their own, these unfortunate people were subjected to prejudice from both whites and Dakota. Many of these people had already gravitated to the area around the Wells trading post on Lake Pepin, owing to Bully's good reputation and his Dakota relationship through Jane. Each recipient of a tract received not a deed but rather scrip that had to be taken to a federal land office where a deed could be applied for. The actual scrip was not issued until 1853. The deadline for filing originally was set in 1855, but this eventually was delayed and was not fully resolved until 1857. The federally established price for preempted Dakota lands across southern Minnesota was $1.25 per acre. The price established in the treaty for the half-breed tracts was surprisingly set at $5.00 an acre by the United States government. For the most part, holders of the scrip were not particularly interested in permanently settling the land, and many quickly sold their scrip to white speculators, who bought them for a tiny fraction of their worth.[11]

Bully Wells's position on the lake was safe by virtue of Jane's scrip. Through her, he controlled the land immediately surrounding his post on the lakeshore. Jane's sister, Elizabeth Faribault, held the next tract immediately to the south. The status quo seemed to be ensured. But in 1852, a settler arrived from Pennsylvania who would herald a new direction for the tiny outpost on Lake Pepin.

Evert Westervelt came west from Pennsylvania with his family, seeking opportunity. A skilled carpenter and cabinetmaker, he found the area surrounding the little trading operation at Western Landing to be just what he was looking for. In short order, he established himself and his family in a newly built two-story store building, complete with tavern and billiard room, between the lake and Wells's trading post. Unlike the rough stone buildings erected earlier by Wells, the store, known as the Pavilion, was built of milled lumber shipped in from the east. The location became a regular stop for steamboats plying the river. The Westervelt family soon left their cramped quarters for their new home, an impressive structure on the terrace above the point, overlooking the lake. This was Locust Lodge, also completed in 1853.

As he quickly prospered in his new endeavor, Evert Westervelt turned his attention to his longtime dream of founding a town bearing his name. In 1853, the territorial legislature established Goodhue County, and within it Florence Township encompassing the small enclave of Western Landing. That same year, as scrip was issued, Westervelt purchased portions of the parcels belonging to Jane Wells and Elizabeth Faribault, plus the trading post buildings of Bully Wells. A total of 320 acres, including the waterfront and the terrace above it, became the site of the new town of Westervelt. Even though the ownership of the land would not be resolved officially until 1857, the optimistic Evert nevertheless laid out the streets and roughly platted lots for purchase by a wave of settlers expected from the east.

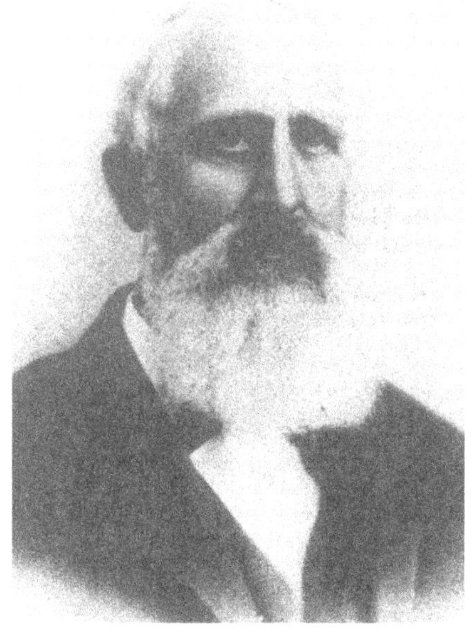

Evert Westervelt.

Arrival of the Garrards (1854–1860)

In the late summer of 1854, two brothers traveled by steamboat up the river with Fort Snelling as their destination. Accompanied by two hired men, they were seeking land and opportunity for investment. As they passed through Lake Pepin, they were awed by the majestic beauty of the widening river and its surrounding bluffs. When the steamboat put in at Western Landing to deliver a load of lumber, they saw not only the trading post and Pavilion at the waterfront but also a fine house, recently completed, on the terrace above. On an impulse, the brothers had their baggage put ashore, intending to break their trip briefly and explore the area. The hired men were sent on ahead to Fort Snelling to await the two brothers.

Greeted by Evert Westervelt, Lewis and Israel Garrard soon were enjoying his hospitality and hearing of his vision for the newly surveyed town site. They occupied themselves in hunting the game still plentiful in the immediate area. The brothers also made the acquaintance of Bully Wells, who was still in the area even though he had recently sold his trading post to Westervelt. Lewis soon departed for Fort Snelling to finalize arrangements for a westward expedition. Israel stayed on with Westervelt for what he promised Lewis would be a brief visit, rejoining him at Fort Snelling soon.

Bully Wells's departure from this part of the Minnesota Territory may have been hastened in part by an incident that occurred earlier that year. Westervelt was not the only opportunist crossing the lake to take up residence. A number of farmers had settled on parcels of bottomland downstream of Long Point, not bothering to buy up the scrip but just occupying the land in the hope that the government would soon issue waivers to those already there. They had already established a tiny settlement called Florence,[12] from which today's

Florence Township derives its name. Even though he had sufficient funds to resettle elsewhere, Wells decided to increase his fortune by buying up the scrip from some of Jane's relatives. Word of this reached the citizens of Florence in the late winter of 1854, and a delegation of vigilantes made a late-night call on the old trading post and forced Bully Wells to accompany them out onto the still-frozen lake. Chopping a large hole in the ice, they threatened to throw him in and drown him unless he agreed to drop his plans for acquisition of what they considered to be their land. Vastly outnumbered, even the still powerful and pugnacious[13] Wells had to finally grudgingly agree to their demands. Later that summer, he and Jane would leave and join Alexander Faribault in the newly founded town and trading center bearing his name along the Cannon River. Bully soon moved farther south and west to found the current town of Wells, west of Albert Lea, Minnesota. In 1862, Bully Wells lost his life[14] during the Dakota Uprising, which broke out in September of that year.

Using his considerable skills as a carpenter, Westervelt had rushed his home on the terrace to completion. The foundation was of dressed stone from his newly opened quarry on the face of Point No Point, and lumber and windows were purchased for the most part in the East and shipped in. Built in the latest style, this sophisticated structure was highly unique to an area where most residences were still made of logs or native sod. Both brothers were highly impressed with Westervelt's energy and also the beauty of the town site and its surrounding areas.

Israel and Lewis Garrard were members of a wealthy family based in Cincinnati, Ohio. On their father's side they descended from early settlers of Kentucky. Their father had served as governor of the state. Their mother, Sarah Bella Ludlow, was a descendant of the family who had laid out and developed the city of Cincinnati. After her long marriage to Jeptha Garrard,[15] he died leaving Sarah a wealthy widow with four sons.

Sarah then married John B. McLean, himself a wealthy widower with a grown son, Nathaniel. John McLean was

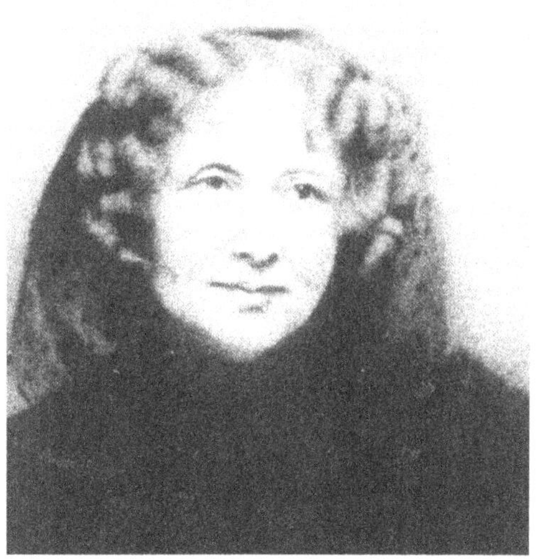

Sarah Bella Ludlow Garrard McLean.

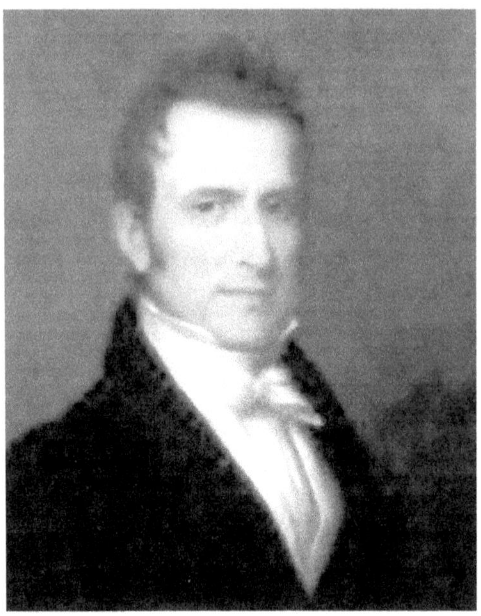

John B. McLean, justice of the United States Supreme Court.

a justice of the United States Supreme Court. Active in the newly formed Republican Party, he was one of the candidates proposed for the presidency at their convention in 1860. He threw his support to Lincoln after a number of ballots. The McLeans settled into residence at Sarah's estate, Chapelwood, in Cincinnati.

Sarah's four sons were Israel, born in 1822 and aged thirty-two at the time he arrived at Western Landing; Lewis, born in 1829, then twenty-five years of age; Kenner, born in 1827; and Jeptha, born in 1836. Israel had studied law and had a small practice at that time in Cincinnati. Lewis studied medicine but never seriously practiced it. Kenner was a career soldier, a graduate of the Military Academy at West Point. Jeptha, the youngest, had recently completed his own law studies and was newly admitted to the bar in Ohio. Because of the extensive family fortunes, none of the Garrard brothers had to concern themselves with making a living and were free to follow their own pursuits.

Lewis was extremely adventurous and had returned a few years previously from extensive travels in the Southwest, where he participated in a number of expeditions and had even experienced fighting against the native tribes. He enjoyed some brief fame in the East with the publication of his experiences in a book entitled *Wah-To-Yah and the Taos Trail*. Back in Cincinnati, but still thirsting for adventure, he proposed to his older brother, Israel, that they travel to Fort Snelling in Minnesota Territory. There, thanks to their stepfather's connections, they would join a military expedition headed as far west as Montana to map and explore the new territory there. The brothers would seek out opportunities for investment in these western lands. Israel, already bored with the practice of law, finally gave in to his brother's persuasion. Just prior to their embarkation, Israel proposed to Miss Kate Wood of New York City. As the steamboat pulled away from the docks at Cincinnati, turning westward down the Ohio River, Israel was a happily engaged man. Knowing that he would be married upon his return, Israel turned westward and anticipated a fine trip with his enthusiastic younger brother.

After tarrying for a few weeks on the shore of Lake Pepin, Lewis finally bid farewell to the Westervelt family and Israel, boarding a boat for Fort Snelling. Upon arriving, he discovered that his two hired men had done little since their own arrival there. After conferring with Captain Nathaniel McLean[16] at the fort, he moved his party to a campsite near the village of St. Anthony on the Mississippi River, a few miles west of Fort Snelling. He settled in to await his brother. The plan was to move westward along the Missouri River to Fort Union,[17] seeking land that was worthy of investment. After waiting a number of weeks for Israel to arrive, enduring constant rain and the ineffectiveness of his two hired men, Lewis became impatient.[18] He returned downriver to Western Landing, where he found his missing brother still in residence. Israel announced that he wanted to spend more time there with his new friend, Evert Westervelt. Lewis opted to continue homeward. After a brief visit in Cincinnati, he would continue on to Europe, where he would remain for a few years. Israel remained in the house on the terrace as a guest of the Westervelts.

Spending hours with Evert looking at his maps and listening to his enthusiastic plans for the new town of Westervelt, Israel made a decision probably more from youthful exuberance rather than any sort of logic. He offered to purchase half of Evert's holdings and become a full partner in the venture. The cash-strapped Westervelt readily agreed. In the initial informal survey done by Evert in 1853, he had reserved six large lots, each a full block of six acres, along the terrace directly above the point. These afforded a spectacular view of the river all the way to Maiden Rock, three miles away on the Wisconsin shore. Evert's house was on one of these prime lots. Israel decided to build his own house on the neighboring lot to the north. Evert offered his assistance, and an order for milled lumber and sash was dispatched on the next eastbound steamboat.

By the time the materials arrived in the fall of 1854, a foundation of cut stone from the partners' quarry had been laid, and the house was completed in 1855. Less formal than Evert's Greek Revival–style house next door, Israel's was in the more casual style developed in the early French settlements. The initial structure was two stories in height, with two rooms up and two down. An airy veranda fronted both upper and lower levels. A small lean-to wing at the rear housed a minimal kitchen, barely suitable for the bachelor needs of Israel. Evert had named his house Locust Lodge for the trees surrounding it. Israel chose a different kind of name for his new home. Named for the

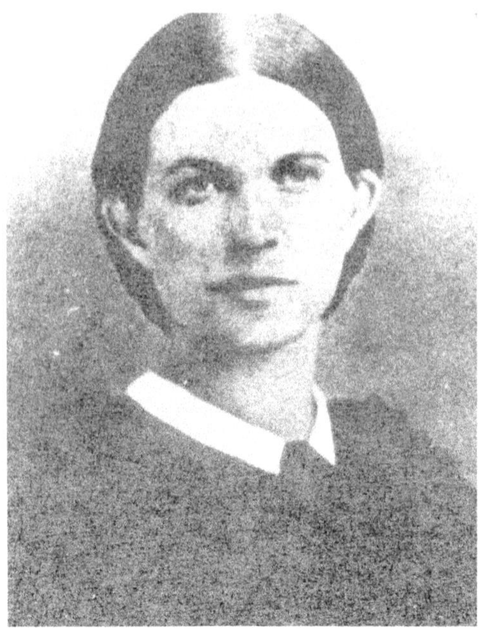
Kate Wood Garrard.

patron saint of hunters, the house was called St. Hubert's Lodge. After seeing his creation completed in the late fall of 1855, Israel boarded one of the last steamboats before the river froze and made his way back to Cincinnati and his patient fiancée, Kate. In addition to Kate, Sarah McLean and Israel's brothers also anxiously awaited news of his new endeavor in the western lands. With a long tradition on both sides of the family of pioneering settlement, his project was viewed with intense interest. Israel Garrard and Kate Wood were married in New York in May 1856.

Within weeks, the newly wed couple arrived to take up their residence at St. Hubert's Lodge. Kate Garrard soon became at ease with the Westervelts and other neighbors who had recently arrived to purchase lots in the new town and build their homes there. The arrival of his new bride, and a desire to please her, caused Israel to embark upon a building binge as he expanded the little house in all directions. In 1857, Lewis returned from his travels and settled in. Selecting the northernmost of the prime terrace lots, he built his own home on it in 1859, naming it Dacotah Cottage.

In 1857, as the deeds were finally issued for the scrip, Israel Garrard and Evert Westervelt assumed full ownership of the town site of Westervelt. Shortly thereafter, the four Garrard brothers would buy out half of Westervelt's share, plus extensive tracts of land surrounding the new town. At one point, the Garrards would own land for about six miles southward toward the new town of Lake City, itself established in 1858. In 1859, Israel changed the name of the town to Frontenac in memory of Count Louis de Buade de Frontenac et de Pallau, governor general of Canada between 1670 and 1698.[19] Evert Westervelt, satisfied with his financial gains, would spend the rest of his life in Frontenac in peaceful retirement as he watched his vision of a town grow up around him.

Another important event occurred in 1857 and would affect the new little town. That year, the military road between Fort Snelling and Wabasha was finally completed. Surveying and initial construction started in 1852, but it took five years to complete.[20] The road started at Mendota and mostly followed the tops of the bluffs along the Mississippi River, coming down to water level to touch the newly founded communities of Red Wing and Lake City and finally ending at Wabasha. One of five military roads that would ultimately radiate outward from Fort Snelling into the new Minnesota Territory,[21] the Mendota-to-Wabasha link was given the highest priority. Supplies and troops for the fort traveled primarily up the Mississippi River by steamboat. The swift currents kept the river ice free and open to travel, except for those few periods of deepest winter when portions would freeze. But Lake Pepin, with its slower current, would be then, as it still is today, the "first to freeze and the last to thaw," blocking the upper river to boat traffic for sometimes four months a year. Thus, the military road provided an important bypass around Lake Pepin and kept the supply line open year-round. The benefit to Frontenac was road access[22] to Lake City and Red Wing, even in the earliest formative years of these communities.

Shortly after the formal platting of Frontenac in 1857, the Garrards began to sell building lots to newcomers attracted to the little village as a place to settle and make a home. Some came only for a season or two, finding employment on the many building projects underway and then moving on. But others came to stay and become part of Frontenac for generations, with descendants still there today. One of these was a master builder and jack-of-all-trades named Henry Hunecke.[23] Born in Germany in 1831, he came to America in 1852. He soon made his way westward to Minnesota Territory, marrying in Winona in 1856. In 1857, he was working near Red Wing and heard of the opportunities for employment at nearby Frontenac. When he first met Israel Garrard that year, a lifetime association was begun that would last a half century. Henry soon took charge of all of Israel's many building projects and purchased a building lot where he built his own modest residence. Because of Israel Garrard's reputation for paying well and his many projects, there was no shortage of willing and skilled labor to staff Hunecke's work crews around the village. Many of these new arrivals also built residences and put down their own roots in Frontenac. While a few of these early settlers were directly recruited from the Cincinnati area by the Garrard family, most were people who had made their own way into the region and hired on in Frontenac. Many were immigrants, hailing from Germany, Austria and the Scandinavian countries.

Others also came, not to settle but to visit. As soon as Israel completed St. Hubert's Lodge, word spread up and down the river of the little enclave at Frontenac, and a number of people arrived at the steamboat landing to see for themselves the grand vista of the lake and to greet the new patron of the town.

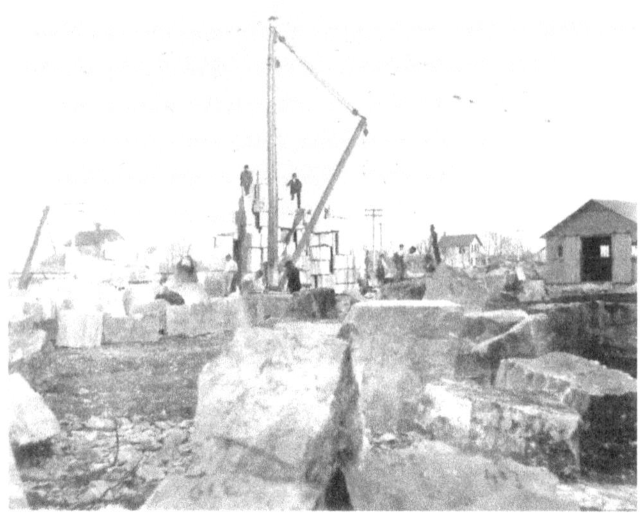

Stone was shipped all over the country from Frontenac's busy quarry on Garrard's Bluff. *GCHS.*

Some knew of Israel only by reputation, and some were former neighbors in Cincinnati or members of the extensive Ludlow/Garrard/McLean clan. Israel received many as guests in his own house, while neighbor Evert Westervelt also opened his own large home to many interesting visitors.[24] A long tradition of hospitality began that would long outlive both of these original founders of Frontenac. Israel kept Henry Hunecke occupied, together with labor hired locally, in making constant additions to his house to accommodate his guests.

By 1859, the little community was well established. Stone from the quarry[25] and crops from neighboring farms went out on the steamboats, which delivered supplies, milled lumber and manufactured goods. That year, Israel would erect a large warehouse adjacent to the busy landing to handle the traffic. The Pavilion next to it still served as the commercial and social center. Bully Wells's two trading post buildings soon vanished when their rough stone was salvaged for other building projects. Just above those buildings, a sawmill busily turned out lumber for the many new structures.[26] Amidst all this bustle and growth, and often at its very center, stood Israel Garrard. And behind him stood a supportive wife who did what she could to bring some gentility to this oasis on the frontier. Kate's only extended absence from Israel's side would be when she temporarily returned to New York to give birth to daughter Margaret. All indications were that growth and prosperity would continue unchecked, but events in the outside world would intervene to delay further expansion. Most of the key players in the little settlement's development were about to be called away by events far beyond Lake Pepin's shores.

Serving the Union (1861–1865)

For years, the issues of slavery and states' rights had simmered in the young United States of America. The union of formerly independent colonies had been forged only seventy years before. A series of compromises through the early 1800s would hold this tenuous partnership together and enable the country to establish itself and grow. With the election of Abraham Lincoln in 1860 and his inauguration in March 1861, the status quo began to deteriorate quickly. Articles of Secession were voted in by eleven states, and the crisis finally came to a head when Southern forces in Charleston, South Carolina, fired on Fort Sumter and forced its evacuation. To quell the rebellion and preserve the union of states, Lincoln issued a call for troops, and young men across the Northern states answered in great numbers.

Shortly after Lincoln's appeal went out, all four Garrard brothers came together in Lewis's house at Frontenac. The question was, to put it simply: who goes and who stays? Kenner's role was already set. As an officer in the regular army, he was heading eastward to report for duty. Both Jeptha and Israel expressed their intention to return to Cincinnati. There they would each raise a regiment of cavalry and offer its services to the governor of Ohio. Lewis was elected by the other brothers to remain in Frontenac and maintain their interests there. Ironically, Lewis was the only brother who had actually done any fighting,[27] and he was also eager to answer the president's urgent plea. For many years, Lewis had suffered from an affliction of the eyes that continued to worsen. Knowing this would certainly affect the quality of his service, he grudgingly agreed to be a steward for his brothers as they set out on their own military adventures.

Lewis's tenure as unofficial patron for the little town would be relatively uneventful. Most of the young men from Florence Township would answer

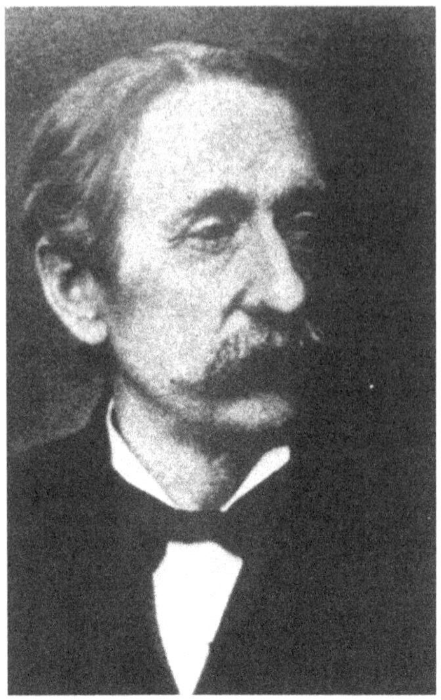

Lewis Garrard, physician, explorer, banker and politician.

the call, heading for Fort Snelling, where they were absorbed into one of the ten regiments provided to the Union army by the new state of Minnesota. Others crossed into Wisconsin to find regiments there. This drain of available labor stalled any development of Frontenac for the duration. Lewis's own interests focused more and more in the town of Lake City. In 1862, he married Florence Van Vliet, a local girl, and began to expand Dacotah Cottage. As his influence in the area grew, he would take on the first of many political assignments when the Federal government instituted the first draft in 1863. Lewis would serve as commissioner for the draft in Florence Township for the duration of the war.

In 1861, Justice McLean died[28] in Cincinnati. Sarah Bella McLean decided that a change of scenery was called for and informed Lewis that she would soon arrive at Frontenac to take up permanent residence there. Upon her arrival in 1862, she soon moved into the home built in 1859 for the McLeans' eventual retirement. This was Greystone, situated on the southernmost of the prime lots on the terrace. Sacrificing the luxuries of her life at Chapelwood, Sarah personified her roots as a child of pioneers and soon entered into the life of her newly adopted environment. Devoutly religious, she would found the first house of worship in Frontenac. In the 1870s, she returned to Cincinnati and resided there until her death.

Kenner Garrard had studied at Harvard but withdrew in his second year to accept an appointment to West Point. Graduating in 1851, eighth in his class, he was assigned initially to the First U.S. Artillery and soon thereafter to the First U.S. Dragoons. In 1855, Kenner transferred to the Second U.S. Cavalry, where he served as adjutant to General Albert Sidney Johnston and Lieutenant Colonel Robert E. Lee, both of whom would become Confederate generals in the coming conflict. He was stationed at a number of posts scattered across the southwestern frontier.

Kenner's war had already begun, even before the meeting of the four brothers at Dacotah Cottage. Serving as a captain with a cavalry unit in Texas when it seceded, he was present at the surrender of all Federal forces and their arms, equipment and posts by General David Twiggs.[29] Briefly imprisoned, he was soon paroled and allowed to make his way northward. He made his way to Washington, D.C., bearing $20,000 in Federal funds that he had managed to secretly withhold from the rebels in Texas. It was while making this journey that he briefly broke his trip in Frontenac and met with his brothers. Upon his arrival in Washington, he delivered the funds to the War Department. A grateful government immediately sought a fitting assignment for this intrepid young officer, but the terms of his parole in Texas dictated that he could not serve again on active duty until exchanged for a Southern officer of equal rank. This was before any major engagements had yielded many Confederate prisoners. Thus, a worthy noncombatant assignment had to be found for Kenner in the interim. In December 1861, he was appointed commandant of the Military Academy at West Point,[30] where he had graduated only ten years before.

In August 1862, an exchange finally was completed, and Kenner was free to resume active duty. He was promoted to colonel and appointed to command the newly raised 146th New York Infantry. This regiment was assigned to the Army of the Potomac and served with distinction at Fredericksburg, Chancellorsville and Gettysburg. When General Steven Weed was killed at Little Round Top at Gettysburg, Kenner succeeded to the command of his brigade. On July 23, 1863, Kenner was promoted to brigadier general and later that year was reassigned to Washington as chief of the Cavalry Bureau. After only one month in this job, Kenner was transferred at his own request to the Army of the Cumberland in the western theater. There he assumed command of the 2nd Cavalry Division and led it throughout Sherman's Atlanta campaign. He then returned to the infantry and commanded a division under General Thomas at the Battle of Nashville. As a result of citations for bravery at Nashville, Kenner was promoted to the rank of major general. He ended the war commanding troops in Alabama and was instrumental in the capture of Montgomery. He remained in the regular army after the war ended and served as commander of the District of Mobile until November 1866. He then resigned his commission and returned to civilian life.

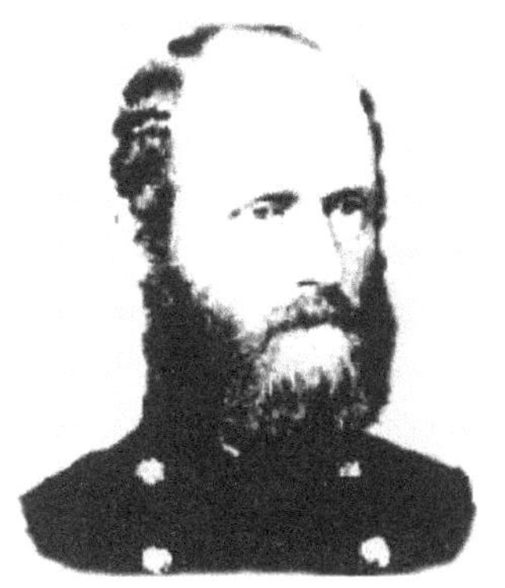

Kenner Garrard, major general, United States Army. *Flies Collection.*

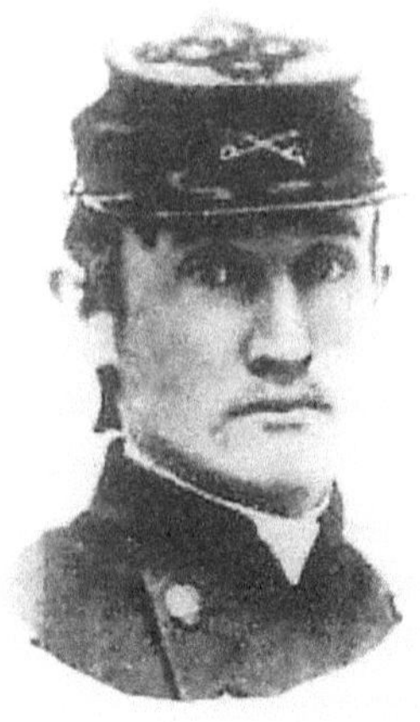

Jeptha Garrard, brigadier general, United States Volunteers. *Flies Collection.*

Shortly after the meeting with his brothers, Jeptha Garrard made his way to Cincinnati, where he assisted in recruiting activities. He was instrumental in the organization and mustering of the Sixth Ohio Volunteer Cavalry. His records show that he did muster with this unit but did not actively serve with it. Instead, he transferred to the Third Regiment, New York Cavalry, where he served as a captain commanding Company L. This company, though part of a New York regiment, was formed and mustered at Cincinnati, Ohio, in September 1861. This unit served in the Army of the Potomac, on duty primarily around Washington in the first year of the war. It would see action at Balls Bluff in 1861, one of the earliest engagements of the war. Ordered to North Carolina in 1862, the Third New York Cavalry would serve in that theater until it finally moved north to join in the final siege operations near Petersburg, Virginia, in 1864. No details of Jeptha's individual service exist, but the many skirmishes and patrol operations of Company L of the Third New York are well documented. Jeptha's performance was obviously satisfactory in the field since he was promoted to major in mid-1863.

In December 1863, Jeptha would leave the Third New York Cavalry and become commander of the newly formed First Regiment, United States Colored Cavalry. He was promoted to colonel at that time. While African Americans had been serving in Union forces for some time, their role had been primarily as noncombatants. By 1863,[31] a decrease in voluntary enlistments and an unpopular draft caused concern in the North, and the government sought further sources of manpower to feed into the fight. Pressure was already being exerted by abolitionists to form units made up of free blacks and escaped slaves and to allow them to see combat. The mores of the time dictated that these units could only be led by white officers. Many young officers, motivated by a combination of idealism and ambition for command, transferred to the new units. A number of these new soldiers would be assigned to General Benjamin Butler's North Carolina command. Butler, a politically connected major general of questionable military skill, was nonetheless an avid supporter of the abolitionist cause. The First Regiment, United States Colored Cavalry, was the first mounted unit made up of African Americans in the Union army, and

Jeptha Garrard was in command. It is interesting to note that Jeptha's transfer and promotion in December coincides with his brother Kenner's brief tenure as chief of the Cavalry Bureau. It is assumed that the move was well discussed by them before it was made.

Jeptha's regiment would serve with General Butler's forces in the North Carolina theater until the end of hostilities in April 1865. In 1864, they participated in the James River campaign and the capture of Bermuda Hundred below Richmond. One month after Lee's surrender to Grant at Appomattox Court House, the First Regiment was transferred to Texas, where it saw duty along the Rio Grande and elsewhere, primarily operating against the Commanches and Apaches in those areas. On February 4, 1866, the First Regiment was dissolved and mustered out in Austin. At the end of the Civil War, many officers were awarded brevet promotions[32] to higher rank as a reward for their service. Jeptha was brevetted a brigadier general at this time. In later years, though entitled to the honorific of "general," Jeptha still preferred "colonel." Many of the hardened veterans of the First Regiment, U.S. Colored Cavalry, would be transported to St. Louis to reenlist in the newly formed Tenth U.S. Cavalry. This unit would go on to garner fame in the history of the American West as the Buffalo Soldiers.[33] Jeptha Garrard bid farewell to his troops and left Texas in early 1866. After such a long series of campaigns, he turned eastward and sought a respite from warfare.

When Israel Garrard boarded the steamboat in 1861 that would carry him back to Cincinnati for military service, Kate and little Margaret accompanied him. The family moved in with Sarah at Chapelwood. In Cincinnati, Israel divided his own time between recruiting a new cavalry regiment and assisting his mother in closing her affairs and preparing for her move to Frontenac. It was not until October 1862 that the Seventh

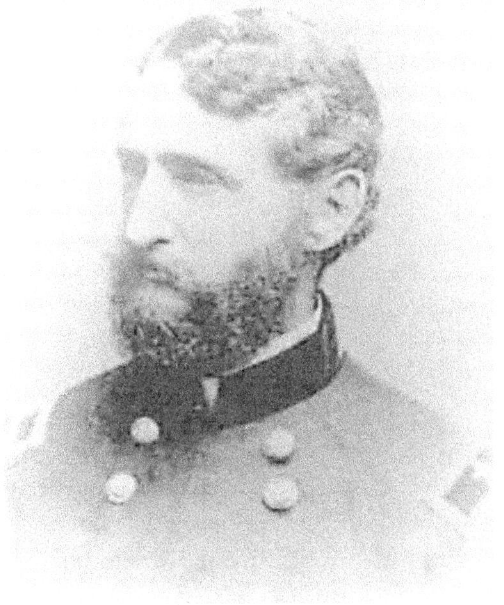

Israel Garrard, brigadier general, United States Volunteers. *Friends Collection.*

Ohio Cavalry was finally mustered with Colonel Israel Garrard in command. As Kate moved on to spend the duration with her family in New York, and with his mother now established with Lewis in Frontenac, Israel entered upon his own active duty. During her stay in New York, Kate gave birth to their second child, George Wood Garrard.

The Seventh Ohio Cavalry would serve in the western theater of the war until it finally wound down in 1865. First seeing action in Eastern Tennessee and West Virginia, Israel and his troopers would be active in a number of skirmishes and small engagements with Confederate forces. In 1863, Confederate Cavalry under General Morgan crossed the Ohio River to the Indiana shore and proceeded to raid eastward into Ohio. Participating in the Union pursuit was the Seventh Ohio Cavalry, and it was present at Morgan's surrender near Cincinnati. It would go on to serve in a number of campaigns as the Union forces under General Grant and, later, General Sherman as he closed in on and finally captured Nashville, Atlanta and other key Confederate strong points west of the Allegheny Mountains. When Sherman's main force headed east on his march through Georgia in 1864, the Seventh Ohio would remain in northern Alabama as a scouting force to protect Sherman's rear. The unit would be present at the surrender of Selma, Alabama, and then remain on scouting duty in Georgia until the war ended. When orders arrived for the final march northward, the men were accompanied by notice of Israel's brevet promotion to brigadier general. The Seventh Ohio Cavalry was mustered out at Nashville on July 4, 1865. Israel Garrard, a civilian once more, headed for New York to collect Kate and the children. They would arrive back in Frontenac early in 1866.

In addition to the distinguished service done for the Union by Israel, Jeptha and Kenner Garrard, one more member of the family served with distinction. Their stepbrother, Nathaniel McLean, also answered the call to the colors. Seven years older than Israel Garrard, he graduated from Harvard in 1838 and established a successful and lucrative law practice in Cincinnati. His father, John McLean, husband of Sarah Bella, died at Cincinnati in 1861. In November of that same year, the Seventy-fifth Regiment, Ohio Infantry, mustered with Colonel Nathaniel McLean in command. While serving with the Army of the Potomac, the new unit would receive its baptism of fire in the Shenandoah campaign against General Thomas "Stonewall" Jackson. The Seventy-fifth Ohio, under Colonel McLean, would go on to serve in every major engagement of the Army of the Potomac up to and including the Battle of Gettysburg in July 1863. Between its losses in battle and those from disease, the regiment, which started out with one thousand men, lost more than two hundred enlisted men and six officers.

After Gettysburg, the reduced Seventy-fifth Ohio was transferred to coastal operations in conjunction with the navy. After seeing action at Fort Wagner and also around Charleston, the unit was transferred to Jacksonville, Florida. At this time, the men were issued horses and took up duties as mounted dragoons, raiding Confederate positions in the area. In late 1864, about half of the regiment was discharged, and the remaining veterans reorganized into three companies, still under Colonel McLean, and were transferred to Hilton Head, South Carolina. Later they were ordered to Tallahatchie, Florida, where they were mustered out on July 15, 1865. Brigadier General McLean was finally free to rejoin his family in Cincinnati. Now fifty years of age, and weary of war, Nathaniel desired nothing more than to live out his life in peace with his wife and children. His thoughts turned to his pleasant prewar visits to the little enclave owned by the Garrard brothers on the banks of Lake Pepin.

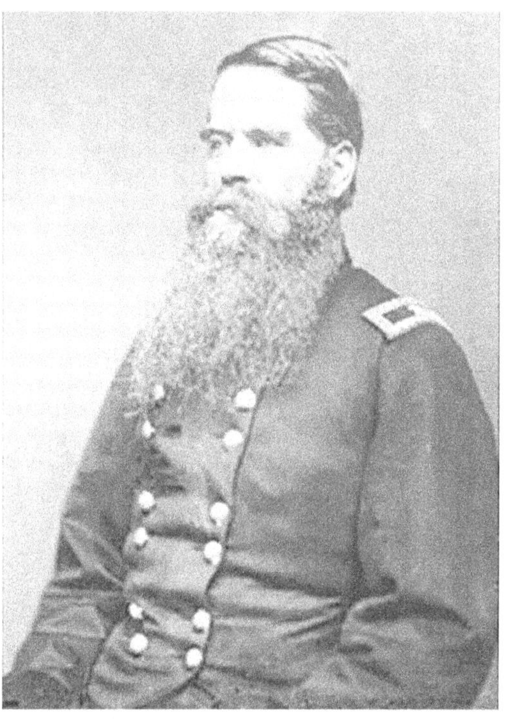

Nathaniel McLean, brigadier general, United States Volunteers. *Friends Collection.*

The military operations of the Union armies between 1861 and 1865 covered a broad territory, from the Atlantic Ocean in the east to Texas in the west, from the Ohio River in the north to the Gulf of Mexico in the south. Of the major battles fought in this four-year period, the record shows that one of the Garrard brothers or Nathaniel McLean was present at almost all of them. Sometimes their paths would cross and hopefully allow them to share memories and news of loved ones. Certainly the bond between these four was strengthened by the shared conflict, and they all looked forward to resuming their interrupted lives.

The Pastoral Estate (1866–1872)

In the year following the end of the Civil War, members of the Garrard family began arriving back at the little town on the banks of Lake Pepin. Israel came ashore in early spring with Kate and their two small children. Waiting to greet them were Sarah Bella McLean and Lewis Garrard, himself now married. Jeptha Garrard would soon follow, taking up residence with Israel until his own home was built. Nathaniel McLean, weary of war and seeking a new start, would come that same year and establish himself as a farmer on land bordering the village to the northwest. Only Kenner Garrard did not take up permanent residence in Frontenac. After his discharge in late 1866, he would return to Cincinnati and make his home there.

With the return of the Garrards, the dormant little settlement seemed to awaken. Some of the younger men from the area, returning from their own military service, again took up residence in Frontenac. They were joined by new arrivals, attracted by the promised employment opportunities and available land near the town for farming. Lewis Garrard, by this time involved in Lake City business and local politics, gladly surrendered his role as overseer of the family's interests to his brother, Israel. Jeptha established his own small farmstead on the northwest edge of the town, where he eventually would follow his own interest in breeding fine horses.

Sarah Bella McLean had arrived to take up permanent residence in 1862. By 1866, she was already settled into the house built for her on the terrace overlooking the lake. It joined the other three fine homes already there, those of her sons Israel and Lewis, plus that of Evert Westervelt. Newly widowed for the second time, Sarah turned to religion. She was a member of a fundamentalist sect commonly referred to as the Campbellites. In 1867, she financed the first church in Frontenac. Built under the able supervision of Henry Hunecke, it rose quickly, topped with a prominent bell tower. On the same block, a large and comfortable parsonage was also erected. The new church became a center of activity for the residents of the village. A small post office and a one-room school also afforded a sense of permanency in this area so recently part of a raw frontier. The neighboring towns of Red Wing and Lake City also were experiencing similar transitions and, like Frontenac, were becoming important stops for the busy river trade that quickly expanded following the Civil War.

At the center of all this activity was Israel Garrard, still following his prewar dream of a genteel oasis where he and his family could live and prosper. The Garrard fortunes had survived the war intact, so he and his brothers were still free to follow their own interests without worrying about where their daily sustenance would originate. Israel's own vision for Frontenac was doubtless firmed up by many nights spent around campfires as he campaigned tirelessly through the war years. When he returned to Frontenac in 1866, his brain must have been full of plans for expanding the village, but one problem had to take top priority.

Though a staunch Unionist, Israel Garrard was nonetheless a man of southern culture and breeding. His roots among the gentry of early Kentucky and southern Ohio had imparted a strong tradition of hospitality. Guests arriving at Frontenac brought news and interesting intellectual stimulation from the outside world. Israel found it impossible to turn anyone away. Even before his departure for service in the Civil War, numerous guests and old friends had made their way to Frontenac, some staying for extended periods. Some were accommodated in the Pavilion, still flanking the large warehouse on the waterfront. But others stayed in the home of Israel and Kate Garrard. St. Hubert's Lodge had already had a number of additions, and the small hunting lodge originally occupied by the newly married couple in 1854 had been expanded into a large house with extensions on both sides and other additions rambling toward the rear of the large lot. The demands for guest space in St. Hubert's often took precedence over Israel's own family, now including two small children. Kate, pregnant with a third child, must have added to Israel's growing concern, but his strong sense of hospitality to visitors still prevailed. Even as the family became settled again at St. Hubert's, more guests were already arriving.

Henry Hunecke was fast becoming Israel's right-hand man when it came to building projects. When Israel summoned him to the waterfront late in 1866 to lay out his plans for a large hotel, Hunecke immediately turned to the task.

The Pavilion was placed on log rollers, moved back away from its site near the water and placed near the former site of Bully Wells's trading post, west of the cart way that ascended the hill to the terrace above. The former two-story granary and warehouse building was transformed into a three-story hotel with guest rooms and other amenities. A large icehouse was erected just to the south of the hotel, near the steamboat landing. By 1868, the new hotel was in operation, attracting guests from points east and south to the cool, pleasant weather of the Minnesota summers.

But in the midst of all this activity and the realization of Israel's plans, disaster would occur to disrupt the family's bucolic life. In 1867, Kate Garrard went into labor with her third child. The process was extremely long and difficult, complicated by a breach birth caused by the baby's placement in the womb. In spite of the care afforded by Lewis Garrard and a local midwife, Kate and her baby did not survive. Shortly before her death, Kate and Israel had donated a large plot of land on the south edge of the village to serve as a cemetery. Ironically, Kate Garrard and her stillborn child would be among the very first burials. Israel was devastated. Now a widower with two small children, he turned his attention immediately to their care. A housekeeper from the village, who already was seeing to the household, was augmented with a nurse for Margaret, now ten, and four-year-old George. Another key member of the household who arrived at this time to take up his duties was a young man named Louis Carlson, part of an extensive clan of early Swedish settlers in Florence Township. Lou would remain at Israel's side as his valet and trusted friend for the rest of his life.

There would be an extended period of mourning before Israel could again resume his work with Henry Hunecke to expand his domain, but in 1868, Hunecke found his next major project from a different member of the extended Garrard clan. Upon his arrival in Frontenac, Nathaniel McLean had gone into farming with the same level of industry he had previously exhibited as a successful lawyer and businessman in Cincinnati and also as a general in the war. He settled on a large plot of land on the edge of the village and proceeded to open it to cultivation. The rich bottomland yielded its bounty, and McLean's soon became the largest farm in the surrounding area. Ever progressive, he would be the first to introduce the new McCormick reaper into that part of Minnesota. A dedicated Episcopalian, Nathaniel financed and built the second house of worship in Frontenac, Christ Episcopal Church. The pretty white board and batten building with its bell tower was consecrated by Bishop Henry Whipple in 1869, with its own small graveyard at the rear. Even as the new congregation began meeting, tragedy would strike the little

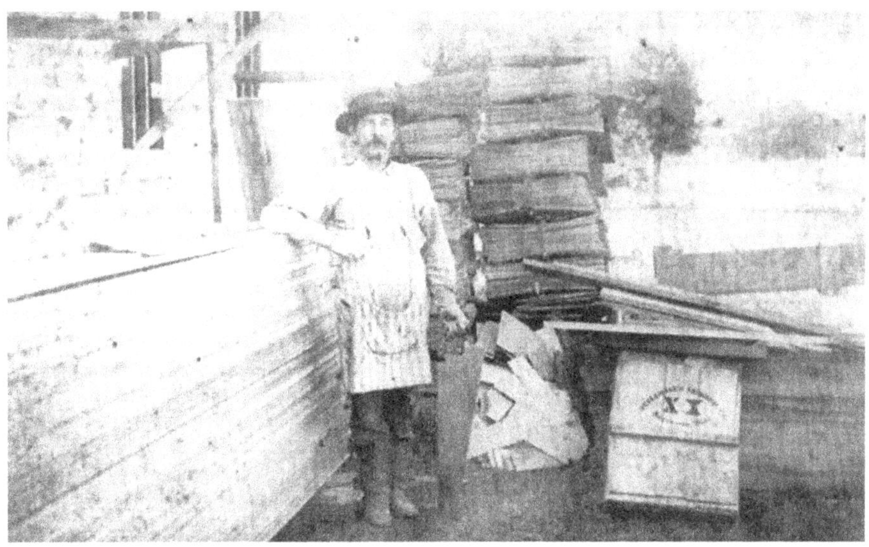

Master builder Henry Hunecke on the site of Christ Church in 1868.

town again. Nathaniel's oldest son, thirteen-year-old Lars, and another boy were sailing a small boat on Lake Pepin when it capsized, drowning both of them. They were the first burials in the newly consecrated cemetery behind Christ Church. Nathaniel McLean was married and widowed twice and had a total of thirteen children. In 1885, he moved to Bellport on Long Island, New York, where he died in 1905.

In 1869, the Garrard family would suffer yet another loss. As the year progressed, a scarlet fever epidemic hit both Lake City and Red Wing, missing Frontenac. But late in the year it finally arrived. Two of those killed by the disease were the two small sons of Lewis Garrard. They were buried in the family plot, near their Aunt Kate. Lewis and his wife, devastated by their loss, decided to leave Dacotah Cottage and move into Lake City. Lewis Garrard had recently established a new bank there and had many connections in that community. Israel, already bereaved by the loss of his own wife and baby, regretted deeply this departure of his brother and the loss of daily contact. Lewis, perhaps to console Israel in some small way, assured him that he would not sell his home and would keep it in case of some possible future return. Though the house was well maintained and filled with the family's furniture, Lewis never did move back. Dacotah Cottage remained vacant for almost sixty years until it was finally purchased and reoccupied by another family.

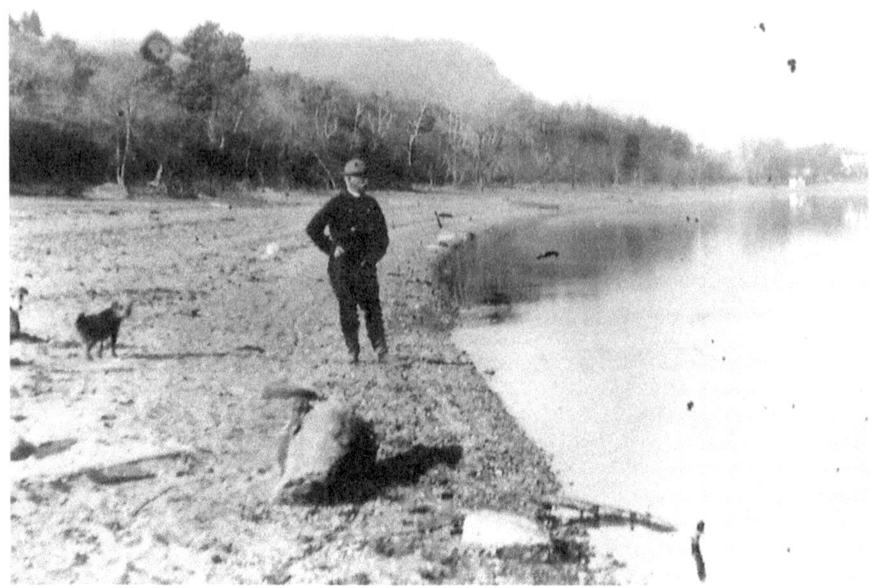

Israel Garrard, patron of Old Frontenac. *Friends Collection.*

The new hotel on the point near the lake quickly became a popular summer destination for wealthy vacationers from the east and the south. Word spread first among the many friends and acquaintances of Israel Garrard himself, but soon others were coming, attracted by the refuge from southern summer heat afforded by the lakeshore.[34] Israel attempted to keep up with the demand for accommodations by moving a number of small outbuildings from his own property to the lakeside, plus extensions to the hotel itself. But not every visitor to Frontenac was there to relax and enjoy the scenery. Others came on business or were travelers passing up and down the old military road from Fort Snelling. Two residents of Frontenac stepped forward to fill this need. In about 1870, Engelbert Haller and Kasper Koch obtained a loan from Israel Garrard[35] to build a store and tavern with some lodging rooms. Of course, they hired Henry Hunecke to build it. Not wishing to be involved in the daily operation, they soon sold the building to an innkeeper, and the inn became known by his name. Schneider's Tavern[36] soon was the center of activity for the village residents. It also became the post office when that was moved from its original small building just to the south. Sometime in the late 1880s, the tavern closed. Edward Westervelt, Evert's son, bought the building and converted it into a private residence.

Another hostelry came into being a few years later. When the Campbellite Church burned down and there was no interest in rebuilding it, the parsonage was vacated. Israel Garrard sold it to a private party who converted it into the Moccasin Inn. A popular eating establishment with locals and tourists alike, it operated for many years until it, too, reverted to a private residence.

Guests who stayed at the hotel found many activities available to them. A billiard room and a card room occupied the basement while a bathing beach plus tennis and croquet courts were outside for the more active guests. Small boats could be used, and larger excursion boats also offered rides to view the scenery on Lake Pepin. But of all these, the most exciting for participants and onlookers alike was horse racing.

Israel Garrard and his brother, Jeptha, were both former cavalrymen. Their love of horses, especially those of thoroughbred stock, filled much of their time. Israel would own as many as twenty horses at various times of his life. Jeptha's own barns[37] also probably housed nearly that many. Two racetracks were built by the Garrard brothers. A small training track[38] occupied an area

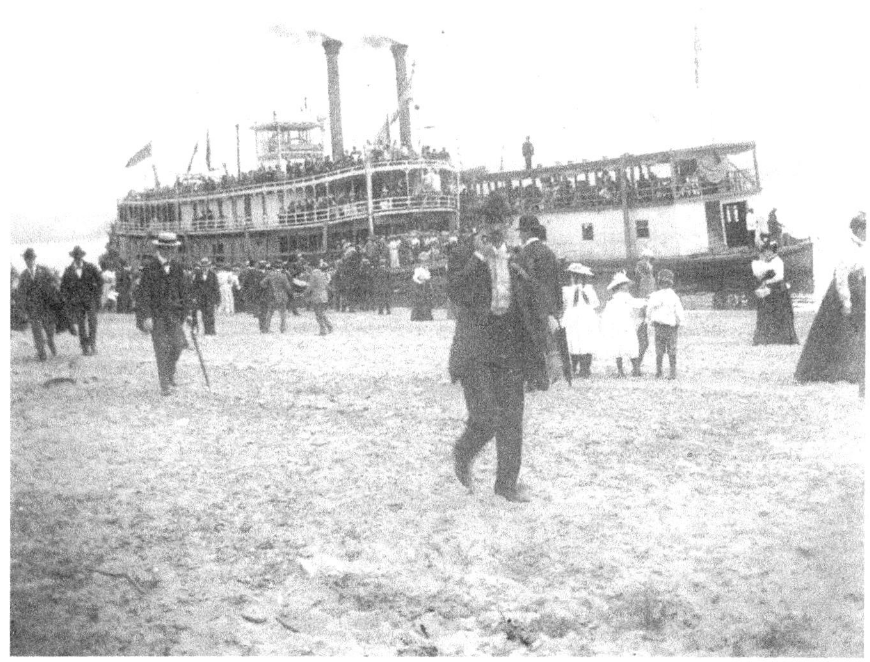

Passengers arriving at the landing. *Friends Collection.*

on the northwest edge of the village, and a one-mile oval was laid out near the face of the bluff west of the Military Road. As word spread about the opportunities for gentlemanly competition to be had at Frontenac, regular races were organized during the summer season. This was the heyday of saddle racing in the United States, as harness racing faded in popularity after the Civil War. Wealthy hotel guests would ship their horses to Frontenac for the summer and pit them against not only the Garrard horses but also those of area farmers. A race meeting at the big track on the bluff would attract large and enthusiastic crowds, consisting of hotel guests and residents of the region. All would cheer loudly for their favorites while wagers large and small were discretely exchanged in the background.

The steamboat landing at Frontenac Point, adjacent to the hotel, was a busy place. At the peak of the summer tourist season, an average of six steamboats called at Frontenac every day. The upper river above St. Louis was different in those days. Unlike the lower river with its winding and twisting course, the upper river was in a more direct course, with rapids and swift-moving water. In the 1860s, the U.S. Army assumed control of the navigation on the river and began to make improvements to aid the increasing traffic. A series of bypasses were dredged around some of the worst rapids to allow safer passage.[39] These "chutes" would continue in existence up until the 1930s, when the Army Corps of Engineers built a series of locks and dams between Minneapolis and St. Louis, finally taming the upper Mississippi River. Navigation lights were also installed at various places along the river to aid pilots in plotting a safe course around obstructions at night. One of these was on the end of Long Point and another was near the hotel on the water's edge at Frontenac Point. One of the villagers was employed to tend these lights during the navigation season; he would visit each light daily to trim the wicks and replenish the oil that fueled them.

Steamboats were not the only mode of transportation in those days that would affect Frontenac. The railroads began rapidly expanding all over the United States following the Civil War. Minnesota was a particular hotbed of this expansion, and in 1872, the march of progress would finally arrive at the little village on Lake Pepin.

Two Frontenacs (1873 to the Present)

In the 1860s, three railroad lines were built in Minnesota to link the Mississippi River ports with the farming centers spreading rapidly westward across the new state. In St. Paul, James J. Hill consolidated a number of lines to form a link with the wheat growers in the Red River Valley. This would eventually become the Great Northern Railroad and extend all the way to the Pacific Northwest. The wheat flowing into Minneapolis gave rise to the prosperous milling businesses that grew up there. In Winona, Minnesota, a group of entrepreneurs built the Winona and St. Peter Railroad west through Rochester and beyond to the prairie country along the Minnesota River. Eventually this line would become part of the Chicago and Northwestern system.

A third main artery was established in LaCrosse, Wisconsin. A group of locals invested in a railroad bridge across the Mississippi and built the Southern Minnesota Railway across the bottom tier of the state, paralleling the Iowa border. This same group of investors then chartered the St. Paul and Chicago Railroad[40] and started building a line along the western bank of the Mississippi River to link the river terminals of LaCrosse, Winona and St. Paul. Land acquisition along the riverbank was carried out in 1871, and the line was completed in 1872. In that same year, the St. Paul and Chicago was bought by the Milwaukee and St. Paul Railroad. This line was renamed the Chicago, Milwaukee, St. Paul and Pacific Railroad in 1873 and became known as the Milwaukee Road.

In 1871, agents of the St. Paul and Chicago made their way up the west bank of the Mississippi, buying up a right of way along the ideally flat land adjacent to the river. The grading crews followed on their heels, and the line grew rapidly. Citizens of Winona, Wabasha, Lake City and Red Wing looked forward to the further growth and prosperity that would accrue from the railroad passing through their towns. When the railroad's agents arrived at Frontenac, they received a shocking surprise. Even though he received the agents politely, Israel Garrard was adamant. He refused to sell the necessary land to allow the railroad to come through the village. The two representatives of the railroad leapt to the conclusion that he was going to hold out for more money, but that was untrue. Instead, he wished to preserve the bucolic character of his little enclave and vacation destination without the noise, smoke and dirt of the trains disturbing the tranquility he so treasured. Israel then totally subdued the agents' concerns by offering them a gift of land that passed about two miles inland from Frontenac, just east of the old military road. Another wealthy landowner just upstream at Wacouta[41] felt the same way and added land from his own holdings to complete the bypass. The completed railroad line thus left the riverbank at Lake City and never came back to the river until it entered Red Wing. It then followed the riverbank[42] all the way to St. Paul via Hastings.

A depot was completed in 1873 along the railroad near where the rural road[43] from Frontenac approached a junction with the old military road to Lake City. A small settlement grew up around the depot, and it became known as Frontenac Station. The original plat of 1874 shows a rectangular grid of streets with names like Italia, Hibernia, Germania, etc. The name Columbia[44] was reserved for the main street running between the railroad and a line of stores and small commercial buildings. In 1876, the Florence Town Hall was built along the main street and today is the oldest township hall still in use in the state of Minnesota. Because Old Frontenac never supported any commercial businesses other than the hotel and some restaurants, Frontenac Station soon became a hub for the residents of Florence Township, bringing their crops to the railroad for shipment and buying supplies before returning to their farms. Stores and a bank joined a grain elevator and other agriculturally related businesses. In 1871, even before the railroad came, a large and well-appointed church was erected near the crossroads. St. Johns Lutheran[45] continues today as a strong presence in the community.

Because of the differing nature of their origins and missions, the two Frontenacs maintained a friendly rivalry as they both went about their business. The original village, now known usually by the locals as "Old Frontenac," continued its quiet life as a resort near the river. Carriages, eventually replaced by automobiles, met every train at the depot to deliver departing hotel guests and pick up those arriving. In the closing years of the nineteenth century, steamboat passenger service along the river started to wane in favor of the much more convenient railroads. Still, the guests continued to come to Old

Frontenac up until the hotel finally closed just before World War II. Frontenac Station continued to be a center of agricultural business until a system of paved highways in the late 1930s and a surge of automobile and truck ownership in the 1950s caused a diffusion of business to neighboring larger towns. The depot and its neighboring grain elevator have disappeared, and the trains pass through without stopping. The houses of Frontenac Station are now home to people who travel daily to Red Wing, Lake City or elsewhere in the area to find their employment.

Meanwhile, to the east along the riverbank, Old Frontenac continued its role as a peaceful resort area offering genteel, rustic accommodations to guests, some of whom still came to spend the entire summer season in residence in the mild temperatures along Lake Pepin. The Lakeside Hotel on the point evolved constantly, with additions and modifications made under the continued direction of Israel Garrard. Henry Hunecke remained the key builder of these expansions, as he groomed his son Ed to assume that role in later years. As Israel aged, his only son, George Wood Garrard, assumed more and more of the duties of patron for the little village. Born in 1863 at Peekskill, New York, during his father's service in the Civil War, George was educated at the Morgan Park Military Academy in Chicago. Graduating at the age of eighteen, he then spent a year studying in France. He returned to Minnesota in 1882 and settled in with his father at St. Hubert's Lodge. Frontenac would remain George Garrard's home for the rest of his life, though he traveled extensively. Israel's other child, Margaret, also born in New York, was educated at eastern boarding schools. Unlike her younger brother, she preferred not to make Frontenac her permanent home. She spent her remaining years operating a small bookstore on Long Island. She never married.

In 1889, George married Virginia Colden Hoffman. She was part of an old and prominent New York family. Israel had an existing house extensively expanded and modified to suit the newlyweds' tastes and presented the finished result to them as a wedding gift. This new addition to the other fine homes on the terrace level, overlooking the lake, was called Winona Cottage. The union of George and Virginia produced three daughters: Beulah, Evelyn and Virginia. The family traveled extensively, returning to Frontenac at intervals for extended stays. Winona Cottage would then become a temporary hub of social activity as friends of the couple arrived and enjoyed their hospitality.

As the years after the Civil War slowly passed, Israel Garrard continued to embrace the surroundings of Old Frontenac, his creation. He enjoyed an active life, blessed with a strong constitution and few health problems. In addition to his interest in horse breeding, he also enjoyed sailing boats of

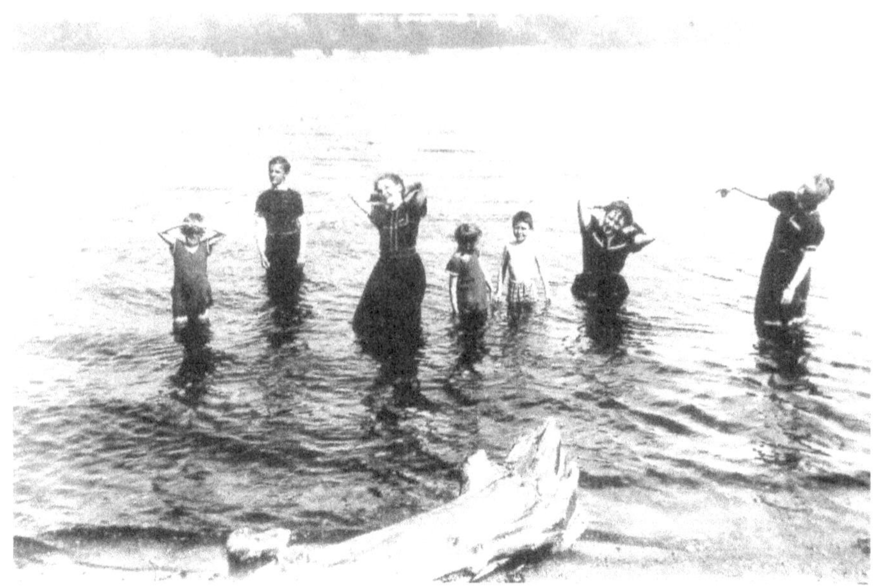

Nineteenth-century bathing beauties perform for the camera. *Friends Collection.*

his own design on the lake.[46] A number of half-hull models survive among current residents of Frontenac that demonstrate his desire to attain optimum efficiency. He even pioneered in shallow-draft keel design and filed one known patent for a particular style he had conceived. Guests continued to arrive and were welcomed into St. Hubert's Lodge, where some stayed for extended periods. Ever the very picture of hospitality, Israel was especially fond of other old soldiers with whom he could relive his military experiences. But his friendships extended beyond this narrow range and included many from the village and the surrounding area in addition to guests at the hotel.

Frontenac was Israel's domain, and he oversaw it as a generous patron. Even after a bank was established in nearby Lake City by his brother Lewis,[47] it was still Israel to whom residents of the village would often turn for loans to build a home or establish a modest business enterprise. When men in the village became too old for other work, they could always find employment with Israel, performing maintenance chores at the hotel and along the terrace at the wage of one dollar a day. Younger men were hired as carpenters, quarrymen or farm labor. Payday was traditionally on Sunday morning, when workers gathered in front of St. Hubert's Lodge. Lou Carlson, Israel's valet, would stand on the porch and direct traffic in and out of Israel's office, where each man received a week's wages. During the week, Israel was a constant presence, moving about the village and on the point around the hotel, taking an interest in all events, major or minor. When his eye fell on something that inspired a building project, Henry Hunecke was always at hand to gather and supervise a crew to carry out the patron's wishes.

Henry Hunecke's single largest building project would arise from one of Israel's most unusual friendships. Israel Garrard was not a religious man. Though not a regular attendee at services, he still supported local churches as an important part of the overall fabric of Frontenac. In 1877, a group of Ursuline nuns moved to Lake City from Alton, Illinois, and established a school for boys—Nazareth School. This was closely followed by a similar facility for girls named Our Lady of the Lake Academy. In 1885, Israel Garrard, hearing that the sisters were considering an expansion to the girls' school, made the acquaintance of Mother Ligouri, head of the small group of nuns. After a tour of Frontenac, followed by refreshments on the porch[48] of St. Hubert's, Israel offered a gift of land for a new school, the site of old Fort Beauharnois overlooking Sand Point. Construction commenced a few years later, with Henry Hunecke and a local crew providing some of the labor. In 1891, the large building was completed and named Villa Maria Academy. The school became part of the Frontenac community and remains so to the present day.

Jeptha Garrard was briefly married following his return from the Civil War, but his wife died soon after the wedding. He never remarried and maintained his residence in Frontenac. Quiet and unassuming, he shared Israel's love for fine horses and kept both of the brothers' stock in the stables of his farm[49] north of Christ Church. He shared Israel's interest in inventions and pursued his own projects with intensity. In 1867, he filed a patent for an early method of using petroleum efficiently as a heating fuel. In the early 1890s, Jeptha became locally famous when he began experimenting with manned flight. Setting up shop in one of the outbuildings behind St. Hubert's, he started to create scale models of a flying machine. Teenager Ed Hunecke, already possessed of many of his father's carpentry skills, served as Jeptha's enthusiastic assistant. Ultimately, a working model was built—a large octagonal frame of lightwood, covered in cloth, with an opening in the center for an operator. A series of linkages allowed the pilot to move the exterior edges of the frame up and down to impart the required energy to keep the device aloft. A large ramp was built on the edge of Garrard's Bluff.[50] A self-proclaimed professional daredevil[51] was hired to pilot the aircraft, and a series of test flights were initiated. All ended with the flying machine rumbling down the ramp and launching into the air hundreds of feet above the lake. In each case, the terrified operator hung on for dear life, not working the levers at all, and the machine glided steeply to the waters below, where a boat waited to pick it up. After a number of abortive tests, Jeptha abandoned his experiments.[52]

In addition to commercial steamboat traffic and pleasure boats, other types of boats used Lake Pepin's waters. The lake supported an abundant mussel population on its bottom, and the nacre from their shells had a very high quality. In the days before plastic displaced it, this nacre, known as "Mother of Pearl," was used for many decorative purposes and was an especially popular material for buttons. Dredgers worked the beds in Lake Pepin from the late 1800s until the 1940s, and a number of button factories operated in the areas along the lake. Some of these clam boats were based in Frontenac.

The lake that received Jeptha's aircraft and the clammers on its welcoming waters was not always such a benign host to those using it. Steamboats on the upper river passed through Lake Pepin with a healthy respect for the winds, which could blow with great force down the surrounding bluffs and shoot out onto the lake without warning.[53] Accidents involving steamboats were common on the Mississippi River in the 1800s. The vast majority of these were caused by exploding boilers, but a few could be attributed to the weather alone. The combination of steam under high pressure, wooden superstructures and hard-driving captains led to many spectacular accidents with attendant injuries and loss of lives. But most of these would pale in comparison to the tragic accident that befell the steamer *Sea Wing* off Long Point on July 13, 1890.

It was a hot and sultry Sunday when the *Sea Wing*, with the barge *Jim Grant* lashed to its starboard side, embarked from its homeport of Diamond Bluff, Wisconsin. The *Sea Wing* usually made its way up and down the river as a log rafting boat, but on this day, it was decked out in bunting with a small orchestra aboard the accompanying barge, providing an excursion down Lake Pepin to Lake City. The attraction there was the National Guard summer encampment of the First Minnesota Regiment, with thirteen companies at Camp Lakeview near the town. Stopping at Red Wing to pick up a load of passengers, the steamer proceeded south to Lake City. The passengers disembarked, many of them women, some with small children. At Camp Lakeview, a dress parade was held by the troops, many of whom recognized sweethearts, wives and families in the audience. At the band concert and social that followed, soldiers were reunited with their loved ones and enjoyed the lazy summer afternoon until the time arrived for the *Sea Wing* to depart and return upriver. The weather had turned oppressively hot, and signs of a storm were apparent, but the captain of the *Sea Wing* decided he could clear the upper lake before it arrived. Heading toward Maiden Rock on the Wisconsin shore, he intended to head

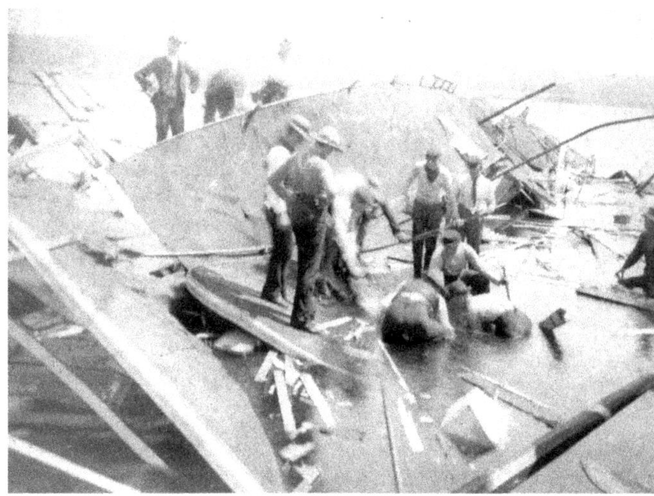

Rescuers search for survivors in the wreckage of the *Sea Wing*. *Friends Collection.*

north under its shelter, but spotting a squall approaching from the west, he turned toward the Minnesota shore to meet it. The approaching storm[54] soon battered the *Sea Wing*, capsizing it. The barge broke free from its moorings and drifted away helplessly down the lake, driven by the merciless wind.

As soon as the weather abated slightly, boats from Lake City, Frontenac and Stockholm, Wisconsin, raced to the scene to rescue survivors clinging to the wreckage of the overturned *Sea Wing*. Members of the First Minnesota turned out to assist in the operation. Of the 215 crew and passengers aboard, 98 perished. The majority of these were women and children who had moved from the barge to the interior of the steamer to seek shelter from the approaching storm. The *Sea Wing* remains one of the worst disasters ever recorded on inland waters of the United States.

As the nineteenth century wound to a close, Israel Garrard continued to oversee the affairs of the village he had created. He lived in solitary comfort at St. Hubert's Lodge, among his many mementoes and usually in the company of a houseguest or two. His faithful friend and valet, Lou Carlson, saw to his needs, and a housekeeper and cook from the village kept everyone comfortable and well fed. But as the years passed, many of Israel's loved ones took their departure from him. First to go was his wife, Kate, and their stillborn child in 1867. His mother, Sarah Bella McLean, died in 1882. Kenner, the only one of the four Garrard brothers who did not permanently settle in Frontenac, died in Cincinnati in 1879. Lewis Garrard never moved back to Dacotah Cottage but stayed on in Lake City. After a successful banking career and terms in the state legislature and as Lake City's mayor, he left for the East about a year before dying in Lakewood, New Jersey, in 1887. Israel's old friend Evert Westervelt remained at Locust Lodge, surrounded by his books and family members until his death in 1888.

As a new century approached, Israel still had family around him at Frontenac. Jeptha Garrard continued his own busy existence in Frontenac. Nathaniel McLean had returned east in 1885. Between extensive travels, son George Wood Garrard and his wife, Virginia, were in residence for extended periods with their three daughters. The old general shared George and Virginia's many friends who visited them, and Israel also joined his children in cultural forays to the Twin Cities and elsewhere. During a trip to attend a play at a St. Paul theater, George invited the entire company to make a brief stay in Frontenac. During this visit, Israel struck up a friendship with a young actress, Marie Dressler.[55] She would go on to gain fame as a beloved character actress in the movies of the 1920s and 1930s. Blessed with an iron constitution and good health, Israel approached his eighth decade with confidence.

Late on a September evening in 1901, Israel Garrard sat working in his office with one of his dogs sleeping at his feet. Lou Carlson and the housekeeper worked elsewhere in the house, finishing their last-minute tasks before departing to their own homes for the night. Suddenly, something startled the sleeping dog. It jumped up, upsetting a kerosene lamp, which burst into flames. Israel leapt to smother the fire before it could take hold, burning his legs in the process. When Carlson burst into the office, Israel reassured him that all was well and the fire was out. He dismissed his own injuries as minor and sent Carlson home. When Carlson returned early the next morning, he found the old general on the office floor, semiconscious. A doctor was fetched from Lake City, and he finally determined the burns to be major and Israel's chances of survival questionable at

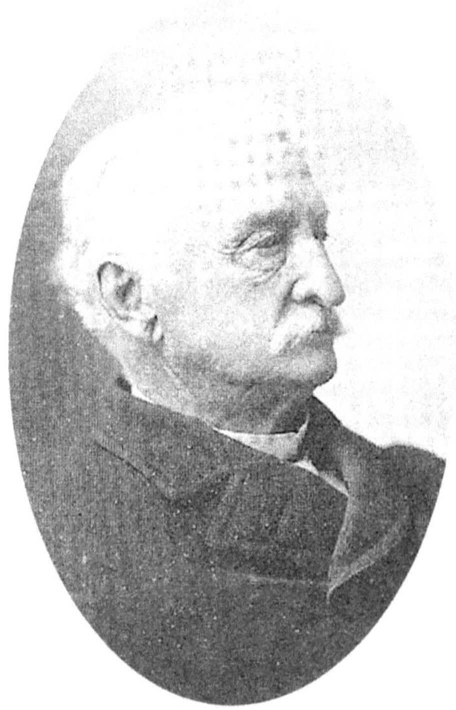

Israel Garrard, in his seventies. *Friends Collection.*

best. Telegrams were sent to all family members, but before they could make their individual ways to Frontenac, the rugged old cavalryman had died at the age of seventy-nine. Following a funeral service at Christ Episcopal Church, Israel Garrard was laid to rest in the Frontenac Cemetery.[56]

With the death of the village patron, things seemed to slow down in Frontenac. Though a conscientious steward of his father's holdings, George Wood Garrard was never as deeply involved in the daily business of the little town. The Lakeside Hotel remained in business and was still a going concern. In 1907, George Garrard sold the hotel and all its outbuildings[57] on Frontenac Point to Miss Celestine Schaller, who renamed the hotel the Frontenac Inn and operated it until her death. In 1939, the property was purchased from her estate by representatives of the Methodist Church. They would operate it as a church camp until 1987, when the property passed into the hands of its current owners.

As the village embarked on its journey into the twentieth century, others of the original settlers took their own departures. Nathaniel McLean passed away in 1905. Henry Hunecke died in 1907 in the little house he had built with his own hands fifty years before and surrounded by so many of the other buildings he had helped create. In 1915, Jeptha, the last of the Garrard brothers, died while in Cincinnati and was buried there. Only George remained as the family's representative in Frontenac, and his times in residence were often separated by long periods of travel.

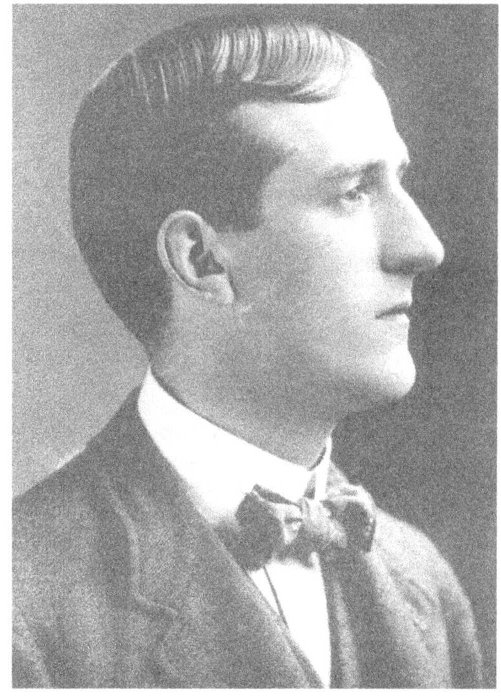

George Wood Garrard. *Friends Collection.*

The homes of the Garrards along the terrace began to be acquired by outside parties. The first to go was Greystone, Sarah Bella McLean's home. In 1910, George sold it to a couple from St. Paul who had spent their honeymoon at Frontenac back in 1888 and had fallen in love with the village. Three generations of this family have resided at Greystone to the present day.

St. Hubert's Lodge was purchased by an outside party in the 1920s. In 1926, a family finally purchased Dacotah Cottage, Lewis Garrard's former home. Locust Lodge was sold in the late 1890s to a family from Boston and is still owned by a member of that family. The last of the terrace houses to remain a Garrard residence was George's Winona Cottage. After his death in 1927, the house was occupied by his widow until her death and then by one of their daughters. In the 1980s, Winona Cottage finally was sold to its current owner, and the Garrard era finally ended in Frontenac.

The little village of Frontenac gradually began to earn its current soubriquet of "Old Frontenac" as the center of activity moved toward Frontenac Station. Life in the little town along the lake slowed even further in the 1930s as the hotel business began to wane during the Great Depression. Residents who lived there in that difficult period remember hard times but also a sense of community with every neighbor sharing what they had with others. The large houses on the terrace were, for the most part, lovingly maintained by their new owners, and a rich lore[58] grew up among the residents regarding the early development of their village.

The buildings survived. The large homes along the terrace, backed by the more modest homes behind them, give the impression[59] of a small New England village. The old hotel on the point, though now a mere shell of its former glory, still lets one hear the faint echo of wealthy guests enjoying the pleasant summer breezes. With the exception of the modern county road, which serves the local residents, all the streets are still unpaved gravel. No streetlights or visible utilities mar the overall impression of an untouched early settlement. No commercial businesses are in the village. As we enter the twenty-first century, the nineteenth-century buildings of Old Frontenac remain virtually untouched by the heavy-handed development that has so recently decimated other historical areas. Occupied by preservation-minded owners for the most part, it is hoped that this little time capsule of Minnesota's architectural history will survive.

Part II

The Buildings

Introduction to the Buildings

By the 1840s, the United States had prospered in its independence. Advances in technology had introduced the Industrial Revolution in the Northeast. Prior to this period, American architecture had looked to European or classical sources for its public buildings. Residential designs were functional adaptations to their region, as each incoming group brought its own traditional styles and building techniques and applied them. In many cases, local climate caused further adaptation and gave rise to regional variations. In this period of American history, few homes were formally designed by a professional architect. That profession was in its infancy, except for some practitioners along the eastern seaboard, and these were mostly concerned with larger, nonresidential projects. Public buildings were usually based on classical Roman or Greek sources, with the emphasis on those elements that caused the people of this new republic to be reminded of earlier glories of civilization. Residential design tended to be left to local master carpenters who worked directly with property owners to derive variations of existing proven examples tending toward Colonial and Georgian styles. A few wealthy homeowners had leisure to study, and have implemented, examples of elegant residences from English historical sources.[60]

As the frontier moved westward, many master carpenters moved with it, bringing their experience and stylistic preferences with them. The better ones established good reputations in a locale, influenced the local building scene[61] and then moved on to other areas when the current locale was built up.

As master carpenters followed the migration west, their own preferences in style and plan were augmented by another source, the so-called pattern book. Some particularly enterprising builders and designers capitalized on the great building boom of the 1830s and 1840s by publishing and selling books of stylistic details and suggested floor plans.[62] These were a great boon to local builders who could use them to consult with prospective customers. Most of the details shown were of wood and such that a local master carpenter could create them on-site with the tools available to him. Other refinements in building techniques also were developed prior to the Civil War that allowed even higher productivity for a local builder. Dimensional standards were established for milled lumber that allowed consistency in construction. Large centralized mills could ship lumber efficiently via the new network of railroads quickly being established east of the Mississippi River These same mills also produced lines of prebuilt sash and other standard components. The availability of standardized components also gave rise to improved building techniques, most notably the "balloon frame,"[63] which became prevalent in the 1840s.

Advances in residential construction were accompanied with the introduction of newer, more American residential styles, each with its own history and proliferated via the ubiquitous plan books. The foremost of these styles was the Greek Revival, which had become a favorite in the Northeast in the 1830s. Another indigenous style was the "picturesque" style, with villas of Gothic and Italianate appearance. A highly unique style was also introduced that featured octagonal plans coupled with poured concrete construction. Advocates of each style published pattern books, which found their way quickly into the eager hands of local builders. Each of these American-derived styles competed with the traditional regional styles and the entrenched colonial designs based on European models. Examples of all these styles would be erected in the newly settled territory and state of Minnesota. Some, but not all, would be represented in the homes of Frontenac in the 1850s.

After the fur trade dwindled in the 1840s, the new territory of Minnesota saw an influx of a new wave of entrepreneurs—the lumbermen. Attracted by the vast tracts of virgin white pine in the region, the loggers moved quickly to settle the area along the northern reaches of the St. Croix River and capitalized on the untouched resources there, notably trees and water transportation. In spite of all the later associations of Minnesota as a Scandinavian enclave, these first real developers were Yankees with New England, New York and Pennsylvania roots. When the first homes began to appear along the St. Croix River and in the infant community of St. Paul, the prevalent style was that which was then most popular in the northeastern United States—the Greek Revival. Public buildings built in the new republic had always looked to classical sources. Formal Roman and Greek features such as massive pediments, entablature and great columns served to impress the populace with the seriousness of the business to be transacted within the building's walls. The use of marble inside and out, instead of the more normal materials of wood, stone or brick, further reinforced this impression of self-importance.

In the 1820s, the struggle of the Greeks to break free from centuries of Turkish domination struck a responsive chord in the hearts of many Americans, who associated their own brief history with a similar severing of imperial ties. All things Greek became the rage,[64] including stylistic touches that could be applied to residences great and small. These were not intended to ape the great public buildings of the day, but instead they were a tribute to the reputed values of the heroic Greeks struggling for their own freedom.

While the Greek style was adopted in almost every corner of the republic, it was in the Northeast that it found its greatest popularity. The style was characterized by columns, pilasters and entablature in Ionic or Doric style. Gabled roofs with pediments were common. For the most part, there was nothing particularly innovative about the resulting residences, which internally still followed the rectilinear plans common to Georgian and Colonial precedents. The real appeal of this Greek Revival style was that a master carpenter, using the pattern books and readily available wood, could easily create and apply elegant details to an otherwise plain structure. The extent of this detail varied with the willingness of the owner and his ability to pay for the extras.

The nineteenth-century buildings of Frontenac are predominately Greek Revival in origin, the style being established by Evert Westervelt in the first

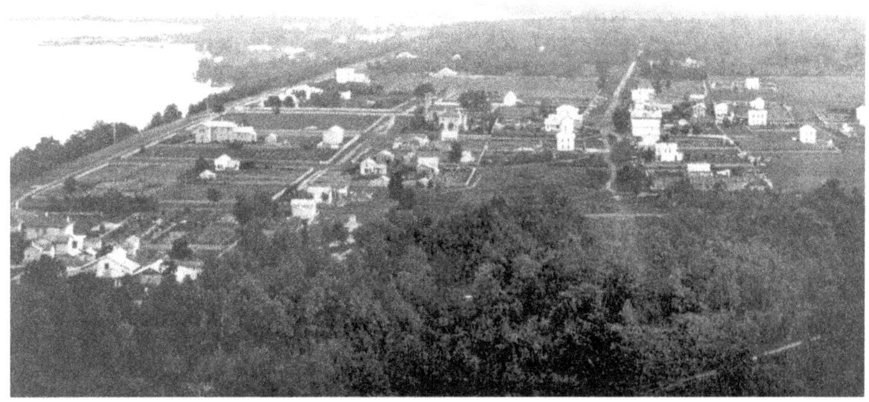

This view of Frontenac, taken from atop Garrard's Bluff, shows the village in the 1880s. *Friends Collection.*

real home to be built there and adopted by later builders. Only three notable exceptions in style exist: Greystone, which is an example of grout construction; St. Hubert's Lodge, which is in the Mississippi French style; and Christ Episcopal Church, which is in classic Gothic Revival style. Many of the Greek Revival details of the original homes have been absorbed by later additions and modifications, but a careful analysis will still detect them. The other two popular uniquely American residential styles of the 1850s, the Gothic Revival and the Italianate, are not represented in Frontenac residences, but examples do exist nearby[65] and are contemporary with the houses of Frontenac in their dates of construction.

The nineteenth-century buildings of Frontenac were not forgotten by students of early Minnesota architectural history, and some of them were described in scholarly literature.[66] During the Depression years, a New Deal program was instituted to provide employment for unemployed architects and engineers. The Historic American Buildings Survey (HABS)[67] was born, and legions of architects began to comb the country for old buildings and create carefully measured plans and documentation for them. In 1934, HABS

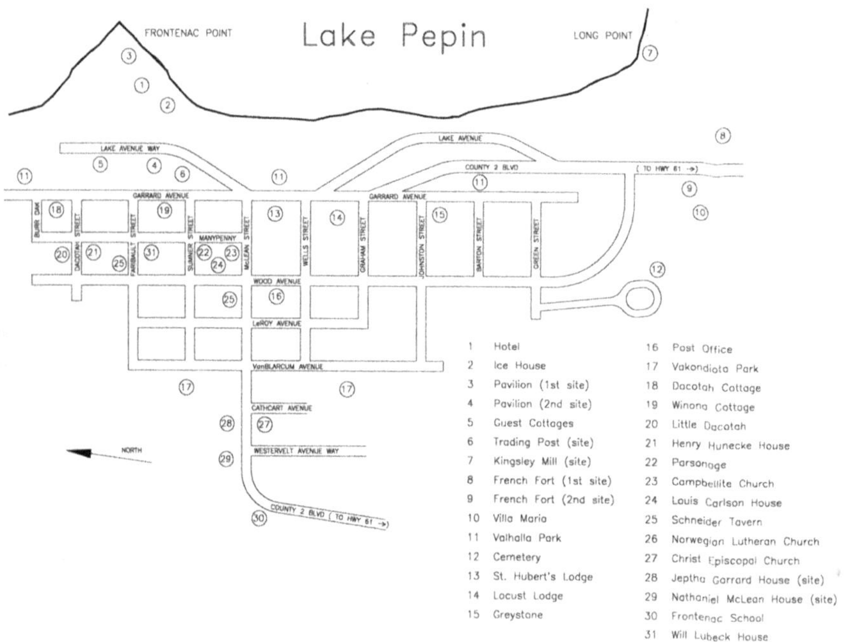

Key to building and site locations.

turned its attention to Frontenac and created plans for St. Hubert's Lodge. In 1973, thanks to a nomination by the Minnesota Historical Society, the Old Frontenac Historic District was created, and the entire village was placed on the National Register of Historic Places. In 2003, the Minnesota Historical Society commissioned a follow-up survey that further refined the known information on the buildings and their locations. This survey pinned down actual locations of structures by showing modern addresses for each of them.

In the remaining pages of this book, a number of the nineteenth-century structures of Frontenac will be described. They are grouped in chapters by general location in the village and its surrounding area, with each building in a group described in chronological order. In a number of cases, actual construction dates are somewhat foggy in the existing records, so the year may be preceded by "circa" to denote this fact. Another interesting aspect of locating these buildings lies in the fact that the men of Frontenac were not only great builders but also great movers. Many of these structures have been moved from their original sites, in a few cases multiple times. For extant buildings, the current address is shown. For razed buildings, the general location of the original site is given.

The Terrace Area

At the waterfront level, Frontenac Point and Long Point form a large cove, with a gravelly beach connecting them. Immediately to the west, the land rises sharply and forms a terrace, affording a vista of the lake. When Evert Westervelt first laid out his small town, he visualized important homes along this terrace and blocked out six large tracts to contain them. When Israel Garrard assumed control of the property and surveyed it for its first plat in 1857, he adopted Westervelt's vision for the terrace. The strip of land directly below the terrace was designated Valhalla Park, thus protecting in perpetuity the lakeshore views of the projected fine houses above.

During the tenure of the Garrards, men from the village could always find employment in keeping the foliage of Valhalla Park in check. In steamboat days, arriving guests must have been impressed by the five large houses in view above the beach and verdant green strip of parkland. Hotel guests could ascend a long set of steps from Frontenac Point to a groomed gravel thoroughfare, named Garrard Avenue, and stroll along with the park on one side and the homes on the other. In recent years, Valhalla Park has been taken over by buckthorn and other species, which now effectively block summer views of the lake from the terrace homes.[68] An arriving boater now sees only a rooftop or two, and Old Frontenac no longer advertises itself to the viewer as the genteel rustic resort it once was.

Locust Lodge, 1853

29133 Garrard Avenue

Upon his arrival at Western Landing in 1852, and following his purchase of land from the wives of Bully Wells and Alexander Faribault, Evert Westervelt began to build. While his store on the point went up, he began the construction of a permanent home for his family on the rise behind the point. Even before laying out the village of Westervelt, Evert visualized the potential of this rise overlooking the lake, high enough to provide a wonderful view but still accessible to the waterfront. He staked out a number of large lots along this terrace area and picked one for the location of his own home. The site was ideal for his purposes since a slight declivity near the house provided a path that sloped gently down to the point.

He began with a basement and foundation of the fine dolomitic stone available just north of the point. On this solid foundation he erected a showplace of a house that announced to those passing by on the river that the newly established village was an important and cultured place to do business, or even settle permanently. As an established builder from the East, Westervelt chose the fashionable Greek Revival style featured in the well-used pattern books that must have been an important part of his personal library. Balloon framing was used instead of the then still popular post and beam method. The house is laid out in a Greek cross, with the longer wings paralleling the lake. Each of the four gables end in a full pediment with an oval window at the attic

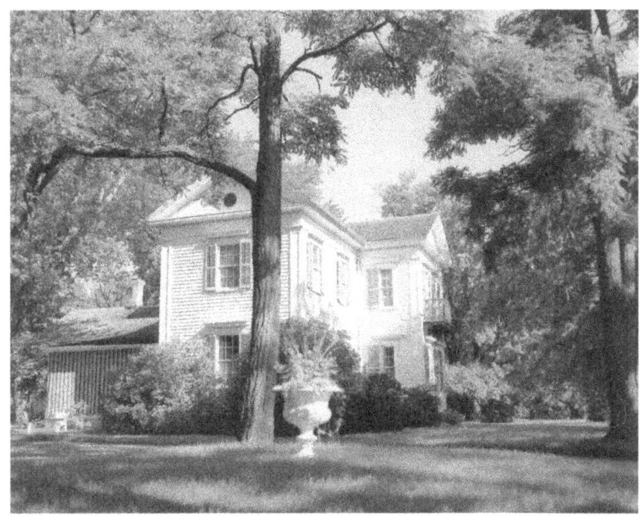

Locust Lodge, with the later addition visible at the left. *Friends Collection.*

level. A decorative frieze with dentils continues around all sides, supported at all external corners by Doric pilasters. The exterior is of clapboard. Sash is of the "six over six" type typical of this style of house. Each window is flanked by louvered shutters.

The main entrance is almost hidden in one of the angles of the house but still exhibits all the key features of the Greek Revival style. A fairly plain door with sidelights rests between Doric pilasters, smaller models of those that grace the corners of the house. A heavy entablature with a milled fascia and dentils tops the entrance. Smaller versions of this entablature are above each window in the house. The design of the house is well proportioned, and smaller details echo larger ones throughout. The severe formality of the exterior is relieved by large flower boxes below the main floor windows in the front wing of the house and a decorative wrought-iron balcony[69] at the second-floor level immediately above.

After Evert Westervelt's death in 1888, the house was purchased by a family from Boston. In about 1900, they built a one-story addition that extended the rear wing. It contains a large kitchen area and a bathroom. This addition

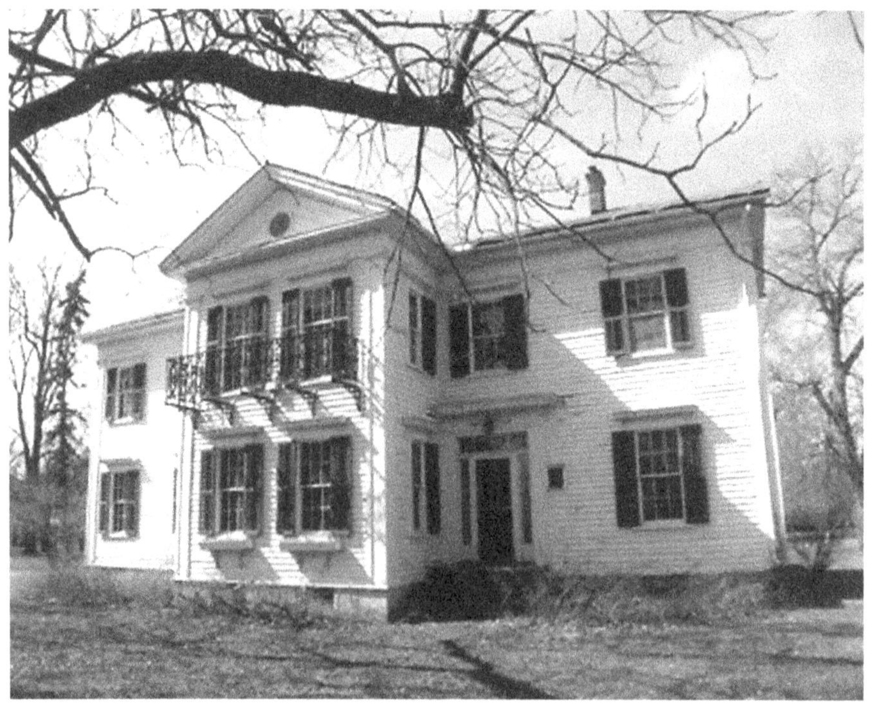

Locust Lodge, showing its many Greek Revival details. *Friends Collection.*

introduced running water into the house for the first time. Other than this addition, Evert Westervelt's original interior floor plan is still preserved. The main floor contains a formal foyer and open staircase. Opening off the foyer are a dining room, library, parlor and music room. The second floor is occupied by a number of bedrooms.

St. Hubert's Lodge, 1855

29055 Garrard Avenue

When Israel Garrard purchased the six-acre plot just north of Evert Westervelt's Locust Lodge in 1854, he was visualizing a much simpler structure than the monumental home of his neighbor. Still a bachelor, he wanted basically a seasonal house that he could use as a retreat and a base for outdoor pursuits, while keeping track of his new investment in land along the lake. In 1855, he completed St. Hubert's Lodge, named for the traditional patron saint of hunters.[70] The original building was loosely based on the traditional style known as Mississippi French, which had made its way up the river from New Orleans.[71] The house was small, with only four rooms, two on the main floor and two on the second. Wide galleries opened off both floors. A small lean-to at the rear housed a minimal kitchen, just barely enough to satisfy the bachelor needs of Israel. The fashion of the day called for high ceilings, but Israel chose to make the ceiling heights[72] much lower than the norm, about seven feet.

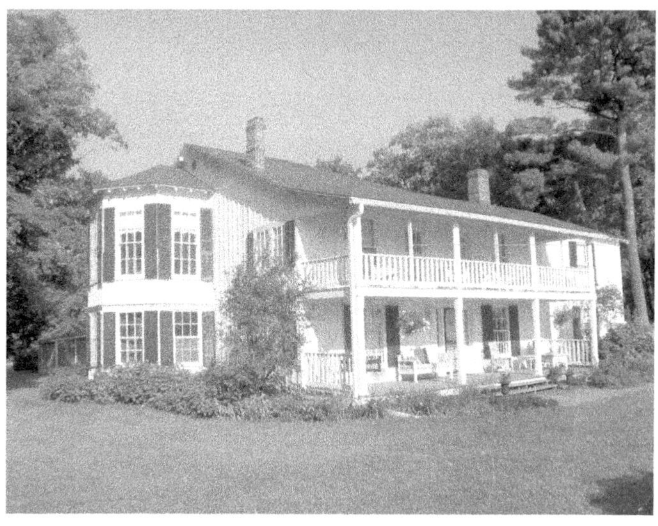

St. Hubert's Lodge, a current view.

This gave the house a lower profile than Locust Lodge and caused it to look even smaller than it actually was. The sash for the house was shipped in from the East and was of a "six over six" pattern. Shutters flanked each window. The house was sided in vertical boards and battens, the norm for a Mississippi French–styled house.

In 1857, when Israel arrived with his new bride, expansions to the house quickly ensued. As his family grew, so did the number of guests who were welcomed and put up sometimes for weeks at a time.[73] A number of additions were made before Israel's departure for the Civil War in 1861 or immediately following his return in 1866. A small wing was appended to the north side providing additional sleeping rooms. A large addition at the rear of the house rambled westward for about one hundred feet to house kitchen, pantries, servants' rooms and storage. At the very end of this addition was a pair of indoor privies for men and women, each allowing seating for three. Another addition on the north side housed a large dining room, while one to the south provided a library space on the main floor with a large bedroom above it. Eventually, the original four-room house would grow to comprise a total of fourteen rooms.

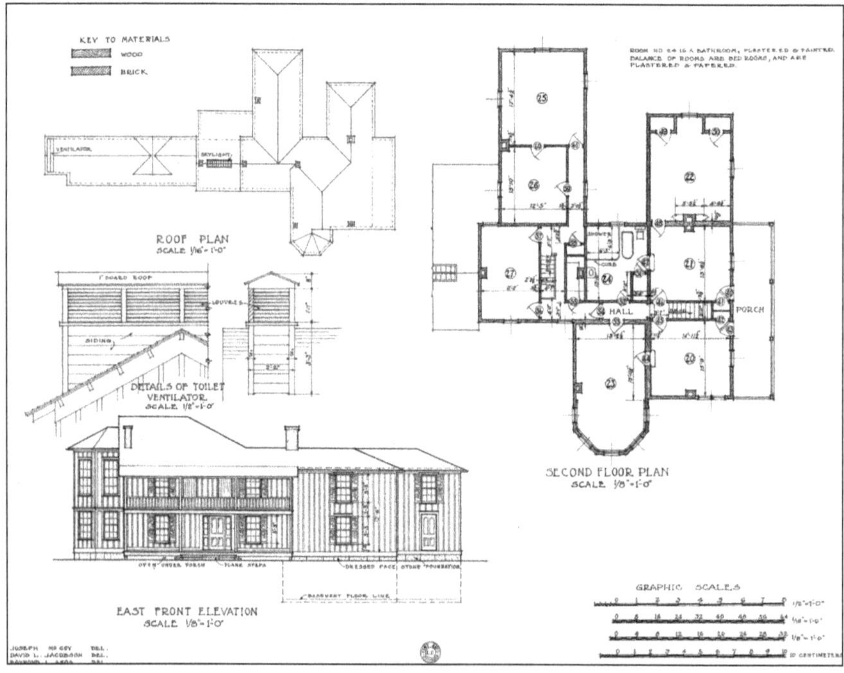

This sheet, from the HABS project of 1935, shows St. Hubert's floor plan.

After Israel Garrard's death in 1901, the house was mostly unoccupied until George Wood Garrard sold it to a private party in the late 1920s. At some point, running water and central heating were added. When the HABS representatives arrived in 1934 to prepare measured plans of the house, its footprint and elevations still were the same as when Israel Garrard and his family resided there. The six sheets of drawings produced for HABS thus record the house as it probably looked in the late 1800s.

Dacotah Cottage, 1859

28743 Garrard Avenue

When Lewis Garrard returned to Frontenac in 1859, he would have been amazed at the transition of the former trading post into a thriving community on the lakeshore. He decided to establish a residence there and quickly built his own house on the northernmost lot along the terrace. It was a simple structure, with none of the stylistic touches exhibited in the homes of his brother, Israel, and their mutual friend, Evert Westervelt. Lewis's house, named Dacotah Cottage, was basically a structure of one and a half stories, with a gable roof and a central chimney. All sash was framed in plain boards with no decorative accents. A number of single-story wings were randomly appended to the central structure. One of these wings, on the north side of the house, served as an office for Lewis Garrard where he had a small medical practice for local inhabitants. The roofs of the house all ended in plain fashion, without end fascias, and had exposed rafter ends. All corners were trimmed by vertical

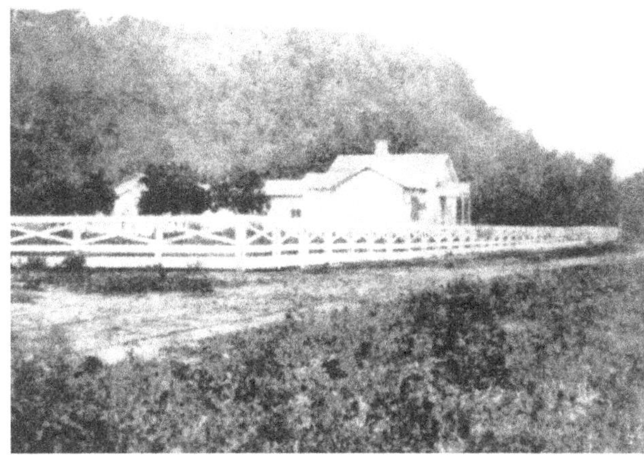

The original Dacotah Cottage, built in 1859. *Friends Collection.*

boards to delimit the clapboard siding. The main entrance facing the lake had a small porch, topped by a balcony with a simple railing. The property was surrounded by an elaborate white board fence.

When Lewis married a local woman in 1862, the decision was made to transform the house into a year-round home for a growing family. The original structure was subsumed into the new two-story house, topped by a low pyramidal hipped roof, still centered on the original chimney. The original one-story wings were either demolished or extended upward to match the new roofline. The original sash was replaced with taller double-hung windows. Decorative wooden lintels were placed above the sash on both levels of the main block of the house. All sash was rectangular except for a few narrow arched windows placed on the rear of the main house. The vertical corner boards and clapboard siding of the original house were repeated in the newer version. All windows have functional shutters unlike the original, which had none. The main entrance also received a makeover. A graceful double door with transom opens onto a large porch. This is topped by a sleeping porch. A

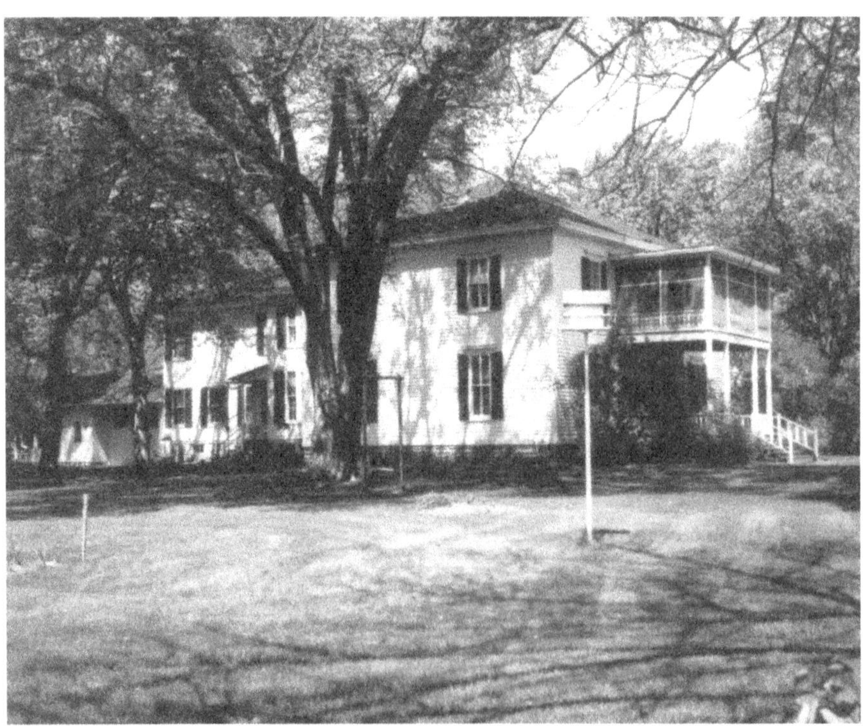

Dacotah Cottage today, exhibiting the results of the major remodel of 1862. *Friends Collection.*

second formal entrance was added to the south side of the house for access to the large yard and garden on that side of the property.

On the north side of the house, a circular drive was added to provide access from Burr Oak Street. This displaced the wing housing Lewis Garrard's medical office, which was moved one block south and nicknamed "Little Dacotah." It still survives as a private residence and will be further described later in this book. When Lewis Garrard moved his family to Lake City in 1870, the big house at the end of the terrace remained vacant[74] until 1926. George Wood Garrard sold it to a longtime friend,[75] who moved in with his family and brought Dacotah Cottage back to life.[76]

Greystone, 1859

29277 Garrard Avenue

Prior to the Civil War, an experimental current prevailed in architecture. Alternative approaches, uniquely American, offered designs that presented options less conservative than the Gothic, Italianate or Greek Revival styles. The most popular of these was a combination of two different, even independent concepts—an octagonal dwelling constructed of concrete. Orson Squire Fowler, an amateur architect,[77] first published his *A Home for All: Or the Gravel Wall and Octagon Mode of Building* in 1850. With almost missionary fervor, Fowler promoted benefits in terms of space usage and efficiency for the octagonal shape, plus the ease of construction afforded by poured concrete.[78] The concept spread westward from New York and Pennsylvania, through the Midwestern states to Wisconsin and Minnesota. As the notion of an octagonal house spread, the concept was also adopted for barns.[79]

Fowler viewed the two concepts as a whole, but they were actually totally independent. Not all octagonal houses are made of concrete, and not all concrete houses are octagonal.[80] Availability of local materials plus builder's taste soon separated Fowler's combination of ideas. Israel Garrard, being of a naturally inventive and experimental frame of mind, probably saw the novelty in both ideas, but the octagonal shape did not suit his requirements. Poured concrete, however, did appeal to him. When the quarry was first opened along the lakeshore, a limekiln soon followed. Here, the plentiful local limestone could be burned and processed into quick lime. When combined with water, gravel and sand, the lime formed a strong cement. By 1859, this locally manufactured cement had already had considerable use as mortar for the stone foundations in the terrace houses and elsewhere in the village.

The house, known as Greystone, was originally intended as a seasonal retirement home for Justice John McLean and Sarah Bella McLean, mother of the Garrard brothers. The method of construction involved first digging the basement and then building up wooden forms with openings framed for windows and doors. The concrete was then mixed on site and poured into the forms, which were removed after the concrete had set. Greystone's walls are about two feet thick at their base, tapering to about sixteen inches at the top of the second story. No reinforcements were included in the walls, though river rocks were probably added to increase volume and save on concrete. When finished, the exterior received a final coating of concrete mixed with fine gravel.

The original house was fronted on the east side by a porch running the full width. A large dormer window provided access to a second-story porch with an elaborate railing. Two small windows, under the eaves, flanked the dormer. The porch was supported on the main level by four turned wood columns. The rafters at the gable ends were left exposed, like those of Dacotah Cottage, under construction at the same time. Sash was double hung, set deeply into the thick walls, with simple wood framing, flanked by the usual heavy shutters. A small, one-story addition at the rear was constructed of wood and contained a kitchen. Behind the house was a two-story barn, of vertical

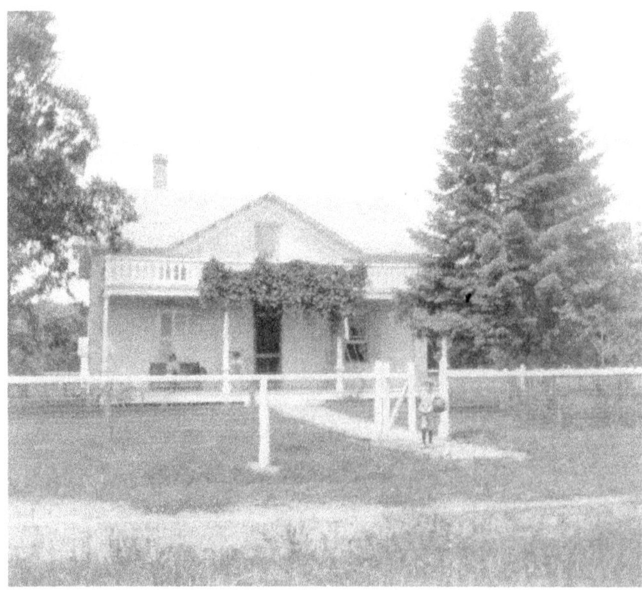

The original Greystone, built in 1859. *Friends Collection.*

board and batten construction, and an icehouse,[81] also of poured concrete construction like the main house.

John McLean died in 1861, having never resided in Greystone. His widow, Sarah Bella, took up residence in 1862. She occupied the house until she returned to Cincinnati for good shortly before her death in 1882. The house was occupied by a series of seasonal renters until 1901, with little change to its outward appearance. Shortly after the death of Israel Garrard, George Wood Garrard was approached by the grandparents of the current owner of Greystone. Having spent their honeymoon in Frontenac in 1888, and forming a great affection for the place, they wished to purchase Greystone. George granted their wish.

In about 1910, the new owner had a major remodel done. A two-story addition was placed on the south side, and the existing small kitchen wing at the rear was extended. The old front porch was removed and replaced with a much deeper one. The large center dormer was removed and replaced with three smaller dormers, extending the two smaller windows to match the existing one in the center. These dormers all end in broken pediments, perhaps

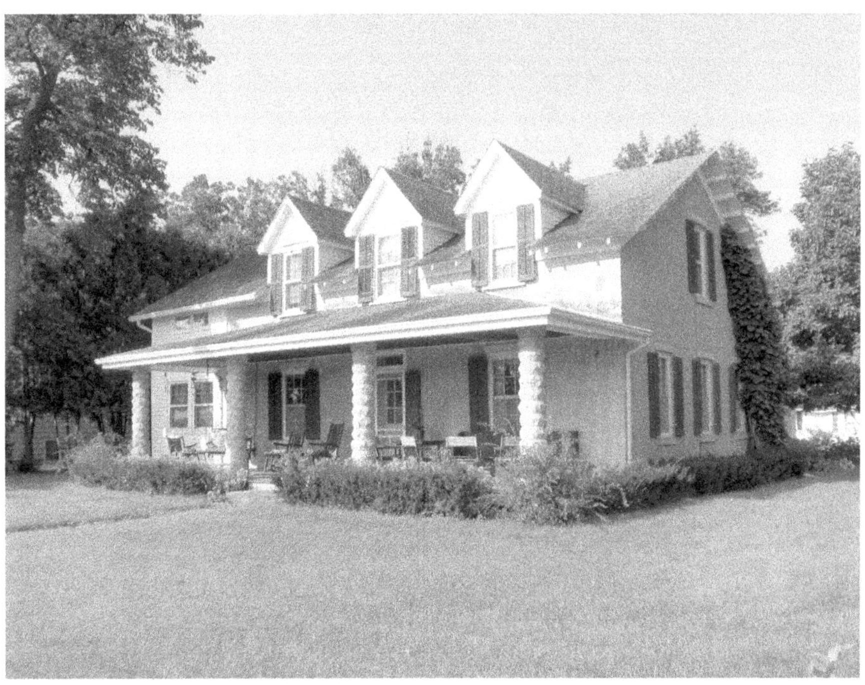

Greystone today, exhibiting the results of a major remodel in about 1910. *Friends Collection.*

a concession to the Greek Revival heritage of Frontenac. The old turned wood columns of the porch were discarded and replaced with four massive stone columns with a spiral pattern. Each was carved from a single block of Frontenac stone and is unique to Greystone.

Later alterations were made. In 1927, the barn was converted to a summer residence, and in 1947 it was again remodeled into a guesthouse. In recent years, the current owner of Greystone further expanded the rear wing, converting it to two stories and then adding a garage, also with a second floor. Even with these alterations, the original structure of 1859 has been carefully preserved. The natural light tan concrete exterior of the main house shows little wear and tear, even after 150 years.

WINONA COTTAGE, CIRCA 1880

28895 Garrard Avenue

This grand Victorian house was, according to local lore, built in 1889 by Israel Garrard as a wedding gift to his son. The story is half true, at least the part about the gift. Actually, in 1889 the current house was the result of a major remodel of an existing house. A contemporary photograph, dated 1882, shows the original structure as a well-established property with young trees

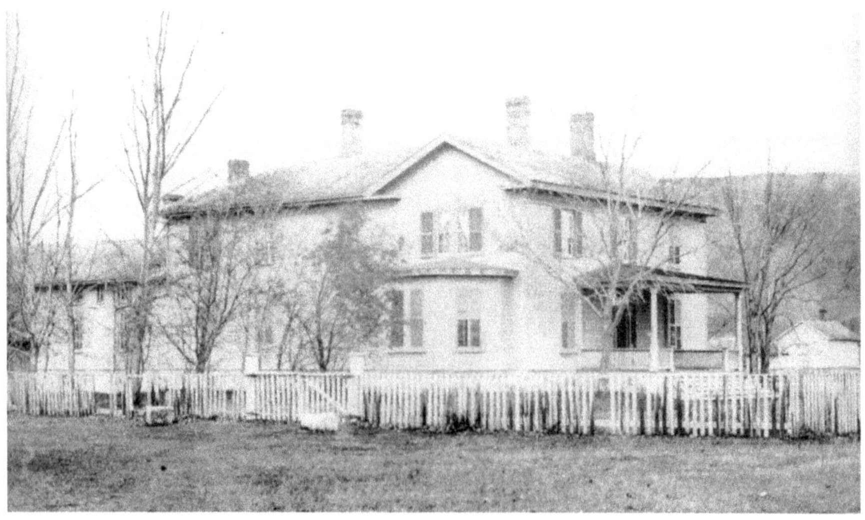

The original Winona Cottage, built about 1880. *Friends Collection.*

and a picket fence. Thus the construction date is estimated as 1880, or even earlier. The original house was a large two-story structure, exhibiting some of those Greek Revival details so common to houses built in Frontenac. Simple pilasters highlighted the corners, and the roof returns at the gable ends formed a broken pediment. A two-story extension marched to the rear, forming a T-shaped plan. Careful observation of the current house shows that much of the original detail is still there. Chimney placement and the original footprint of the original house are also preserved.

The 1889 remodel was done to the specifications of George Wood Garrard and his new bride, Virginia Hoffman Garrard. They named the house Winona Cottage in memory of the legendary Indian princess who leapt from Maiden Rock across Lake Pepin rather than agree to an arranged marriage.[82] The remodel resulted in a number of extensions to the existing structure. The original large bay on the south side was expanded to two stories, and two smaller bays, matching it in style, were built along the south wall. A roomy polygonal porch was added at the southeast corner, featuring decorative arches supported by simple Doric columns. The flat-porched roof serves as a veranda overlooking the lake, surrounded by a railing. The original front entrance is preserved, but the old entry porch was expanded and a sleeping porch added above. A second entrance, at the northeast corner, is in an added one-story wing. The arches of its small porch evoke those on the southeast porch but are of a lighter, lacy design. The original Greek Revival roof returns

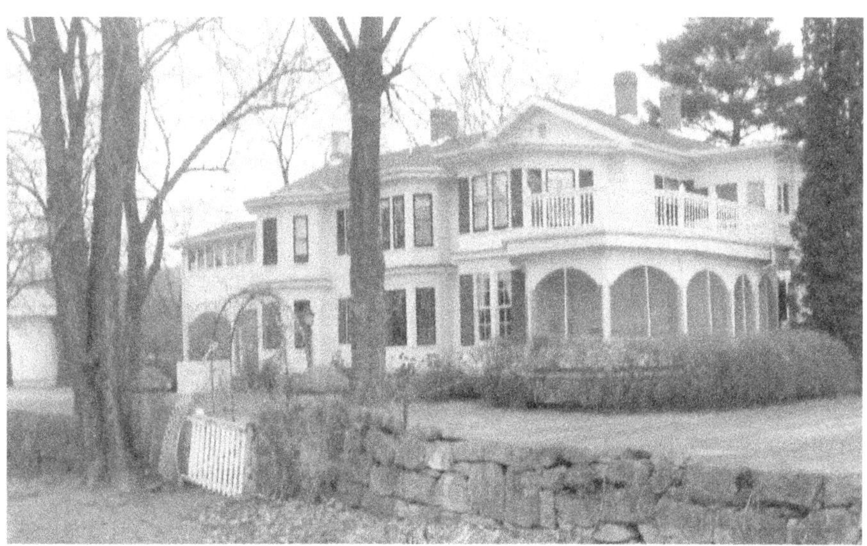

Winona Cottage today, exhibiting the major remodel done in 1889. *Flies Collection.*

are particularly visible above this wing. On the north side of the house, the lines of the original house are for the most part unchanged, except for two cantilevered, polygonal bay windows at the second-floor level. In 1895, a stone wall was built completely around the property, a striking example of cowan masonry[83] that still exists today.

At the very rear of the house, on the west end, a later modification was made in 1958. To form a sort of porte-cochère, the entire second story was removed, roof and all. The first story was jacked up to form a new second level, with strip windows on the south and north sides and a wide, shallow bay window on the west end. A new roof was built, and latticework arches were added below, repeating those at the northeast corner of the house. The original second story was not discarded but was moved to the east, just across Manypenny Avenue, where it is now a private residence.

George Wood Garrard often referred to Winona Cottage as his "Fontana-style" house. Rather than a specific formal style, he was instead referring to the small resort community of Fontana[84] on Lake Geneva, north of Chicago in southernmost Wisconsin. As a member of a socially prominent family, during his student days in Chicago, he would have been a guest in a number of the fine summer homes in Fontana. When it came time to create his own residence overlooking Lake Pepin, he remembered Fontana and used it as his inspiration.

Frontenac Point

Originally called Waconia by the Dakota and Western Landing by early settlers, the point jutting out into the lake was finally named Frontenac Point when the village above it took that name. The first owner, in the modern sense, was James "Bully" Wells by virtue of the scrip held by his wife, Jane. In 1853, Evert Westervelt acquired the point and, a year later, Israel Garrard. The land remained in the Garrard family until 1907, when it was purchased by Miss Celestine Schaller. In 1939, it was acquired by the Methodist Church. The property passed into the hands of its current owner in 1987.

Over the years, access to the point has evolved. On the original plat of 1857, a road was laid out that followed a natural declivity down to the point, north of today's McLean Street. This road, named Waconia Avenue, served as the main access to the hotel until it was washed away by a flash flood in the 1930s. The spill from this flood created another, smaller point now called Carnelian Point. In addition to the main road, a narrow cart way led up to Locust Lodge on the terrace above. This has now been absorbed into Lake Avenue Way, which follows the lakeshore below Valhalla Park. The other access from the point to the terrace was a long wooden staircase built in the 1870s and now vanished.

TRADING POST, 1837 (RAZED CIRCA 1854)

(West of current Lake Avenue Way, near boat landing)

Frontenac Point with its adjacent cove has been a favorite camping place of native people for centuries. Easy to reach by water or land, it afforded an ideal site for trading and seasonal camping. In 1837, the first permanent white settler arrived and set up a trading post on the point. James "Bully" Wells built two structures of rough river rock: a small storehouse for furs and trade goods and a larger building containing quarters for the workers and the Wells family, plus a trading room. Log rafters supported a roof of roughly split wood shingles. Window openings were probably unglazed with heavy shutters to keep out trespassers and the severe winter weather.

The post was operated by Wells until 1853, when the point and its buildings were purchased by Evert Westervelt. Within a few years, eclipsed by newer buildings on the point and rendered obsolete by a dying fur trade, the two post buildings disappeared. Probably cannibalized of their stone for other building projects, only traces of their foundations exist today.

PAVILION, 1853 (RAZED 1976)

(West of current Lake Avenue Way, near boat landing)

This was the first structure built by Evert Westervelt after his acquisition of the land making up Frontenac Point. The Pavilion served as a general store and lodgings for early travelers arriving by steamboat at the nearby landing. In addition to the store, the main floor contained a tavern and billiard room. The second floor provided sleeping quarters for travelers. The Westervelt family probably also resided there briefly in 1853 while their permanent home was erected on the terrace above the point.

Construction was of milled lumber, shipped in by steamboat. The exterior was clapboard with a simple pitched roof. Dormers lined both sides to admit light and air. All openings were glazed, with double-hung sash. Heavy shutters provided security and shelter from the weather. A simple entrance door near one end of the building provided access to a stair hall to the second floor, plus entrance into the store and tavern area.

The Pavilion was initially constructed in the central area of the point, but when the granary was converted to a hotel in 1868, the Pavilion was moved back from

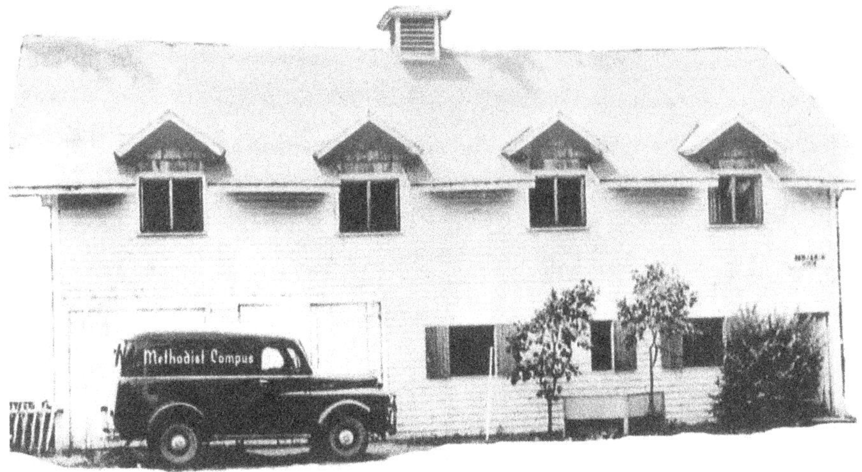

The old Pavilion, renamed Benjamin by the Methodist Church in 1939. *Flies Collection.*

the waterfront to a new site west of Lake Avenue. It served various functions as a service annex to the hotel until the hotel itself was acquired by the Methodist Church and converted to a summer camp. The Pavilion was then renamed Benjamin and continued to serve various functions. It was razed in about 1976.

Lakeside Hotel, 1859

28822 Lake Avenue Way

This building was originally constructed as a two-story granary and warehouse, built in the sturdy post and beam tradition with clapboard siding atop a full basement. In 1867, owner Israel Garrard embarked on a major project to convert it to a hotel. Builder Henry Hunecke, probably seeking high ceilings on the main floor, temporarily jacked up the entire building and constructed the main floor below it. The resulting three-story structure was completed in 1868 and opened as the Lakeside Hotel.

Guests flocked to the new summer destination, arriving and departing by a newly improved steamboat landing. The building underwent many modifications in the 1800s. The first veranda, built in 1868 on the east side, was soon doubled in size, and an additional veranda was added on the north side. A two-story extension, housing additional guest rooms and services, was added to the west end in the 1870s. The original basement of Frontenac stone contained a billiard room and a card room and was the exclusive domain of

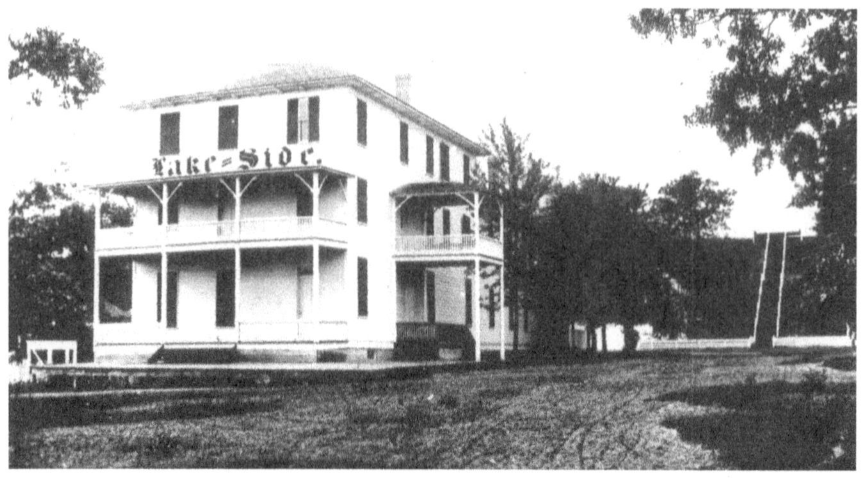

The Lakeside Hotel, as originally created from the old granary. Note the stairway to the terrace above. *Friends Collection.*

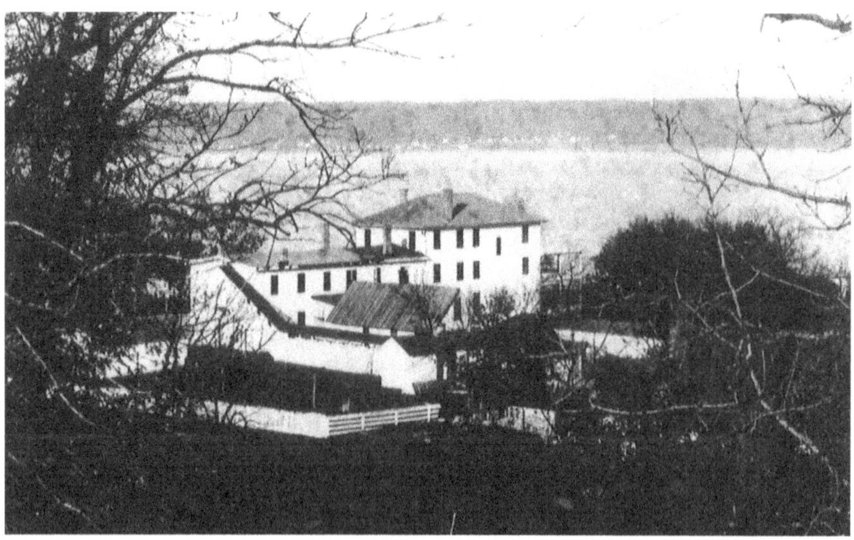

The Lakeside Hotel, after many additions, probably taken in the 1880s. *Friends Collection.*

male guests. The Lakeside Hotel operated as a seasonal resort, opening in the late spring and closing in the fall, until 1907.

As part of his father's estate, George Wood Garrard sold the entire point and its buildings to Celestine Schaller. She renamed the hotel the Frontenac Inn

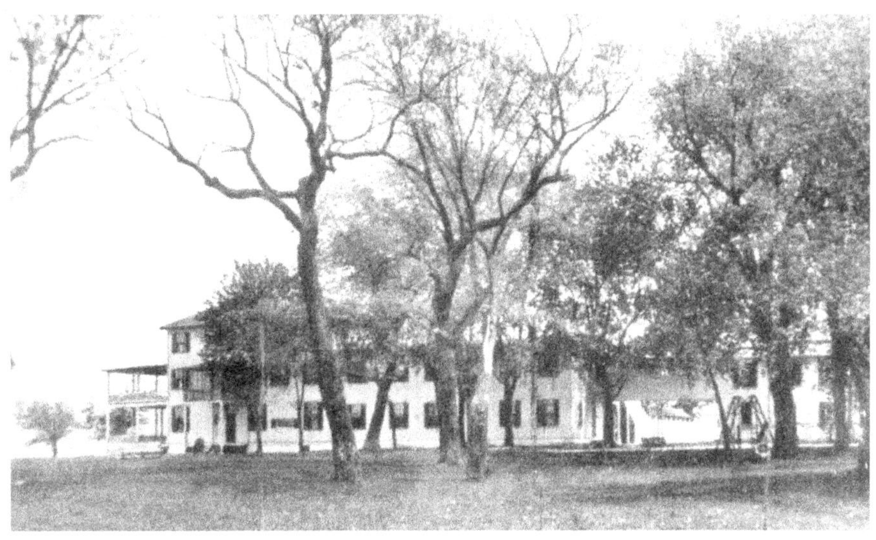

Now called the Frontenac Inn, the hotel as it appeared in the 1930s. *Friends Collection.*

and operated it until her death in the late 1930s. Few, if any, modifications were made to the hotel building during her tenure. Miss Schaller's Frontenac Inn became famous for her chicken dinners, and especially on Sundays, the hotel restaurant was crammed with customers. These ranged from local residents to wealthy yachtsmen,[85] who tied up at the boat landing to enjoy a meal.

In 1939, a consortium of Methodist churches purchased the point and its buildings from Miss Schaller's estate and established a summer camp on the property. Few actual modifications were made to the old hotel, which then served as a hub of activity for the young campers. It is assumed, however, that the billiard and card rooms in the basement were quickly converted to serve more wholesome activities. In the 1970s, as the church camp was phased out, the point and its buildings passed into private ownership.

Ice House, circa 1860

28822 Lake Avenue Way

Before electricity arrived in Frontenac in the 1930s, ice was a valuable commodity. The hotel, the large homes on the terrace and the smaller homes elsewhere in the village required a way to cool and preserve perishable food during the warm months of the year. Fortunately, in an average winter, Lake

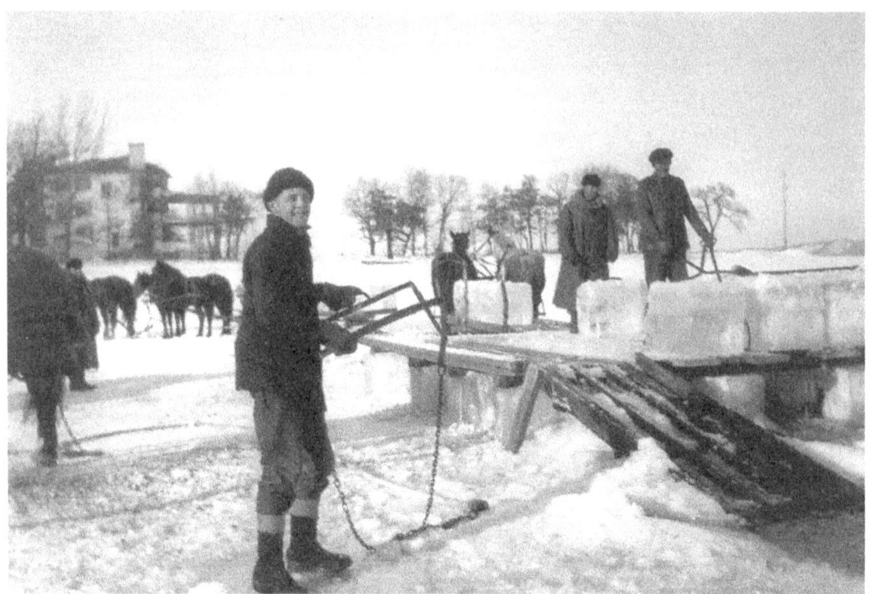

Members of the community turn out to harvest ice on Lake Pepin. *Friends Collection.*

Pepin freezes to a thickness of two feet or more. This bounty could be harvested and preserved for later use. To provide a reliable supply of ice for use in the hotel and elsewhere about the village, Israel Garrard had a large icehouse built. Located near the waterfront for ease of access during the annual ice harvest, it was filled with cakes of ice in layers, separated by sawdust, ready for use during the summer.

No images survive of the original structure, but its probable form can be inferred from similar structures of the period.[86] A deep basement supported a main building, supported inside by large posts and cross beams. There were no floor joists, creating an open space within. The inside walls were finished with rough lumber, with insulation (usually moss) filling the space between the walls. An outside ramp allowed the cakes of ice to be skidded to the basement level. Openings would be limited to heavy access doors at various levels. The original size of this icehouse was approximately thirty by thirty feet. Use of the stored ice was available to every resident, and all participated in the annual harvest.

When the Methodist Church purchased the property in 1939, the icehouse was converted to a two-story building. The original basement was preserved, but the size of the building above was expanded to thirty feet by fifty feet. The renovation was done by volunteer labor, consisting of clergy from the area

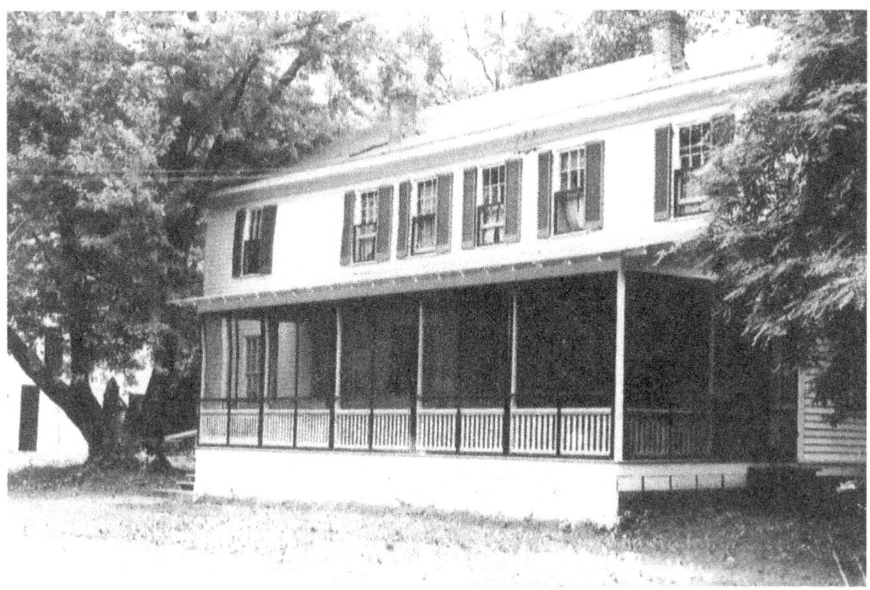

Pepin Hall, built around the old icehouse by the Methodist Church in 1939. *Flies Collection.*

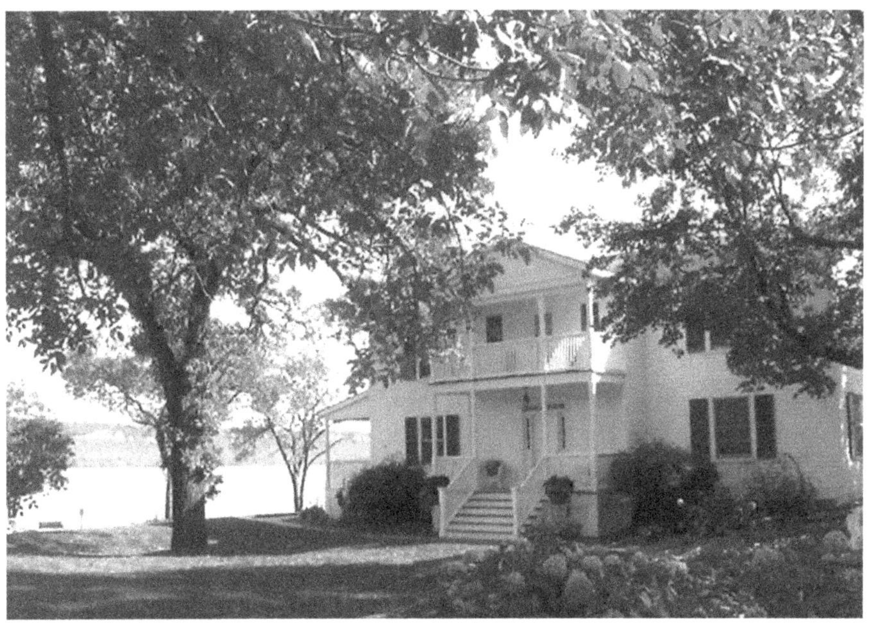

Pepin House, the current evolution of the old icehouse.

and their friends. The lumber for the project was salvaged from old, unused Methodist churches in the area. The building was fitted out as a dormitory with six bedrooms on the second floor and three on the first, with communal bathrooms and showers. At the west end of the first floor was a large meeting room. When finished, the building was named Pepin Hall.

When the property was purchased by its current owner in 1987, the old icehouse was further transformed. In 1988, the old walkout basement was converted, and the grade was elevated around the building to provide for flood protection. Later, in 1996, the old building underwent a total renovation and was reborn as a bed-and-breakfast. Only the framework and the hardwood floors were preserved. The exterior was rebuilt, following the same style as other period homes in the village but with a fully modernized interior with luxury suites featuring fireplaces and whirlpool baths. Large verandas were added to take advantage of the views of the lake. Renamed the Pepin House, the building was a bed-and-breakfast for five years. It is now the private residence of the current owner.

GUEST COTTAGES, MOVED TO SITE CIRCA 1880

28822 Lake Avenue Way

In about 1880, when the Lakeside Hotel's popularity with summer visitors exceeded its capacity, Israel Garrard solved the problem. He moved an assortment of existing buildings from around the village and sited them in a row, north of the old Pavilion on Frontenac Point. Placed on stout posts in lieu of more permanent foundations, they were modified to serve as guest cottages. The cottages contained only bedrooms, and all meals were taken in the main hotel. None of the cottages had running water, and outhouses served as toilets. Each of the five rustic buildings was given a distinctive name. Just north of the Pavilion was Grapevine, then Virginia, Pine, Poplar and, finally, Fern. Grapevine and Virginia were both originally family homes from the village. Pine, Poplar and Fern were outbuildings from St. Hubert's Lodge.

The guest cottages continued to serve as accommodations for hotel guests and, after 1939, as dormitories for the Methodist Church Camp. The church added bathrooms and electricity to the buildings in 1940. After the properties on Frontenac Point were purchased by the current owner in 1987, Grapevine was fully remodeled and given a modern interior, while preserving its exterior

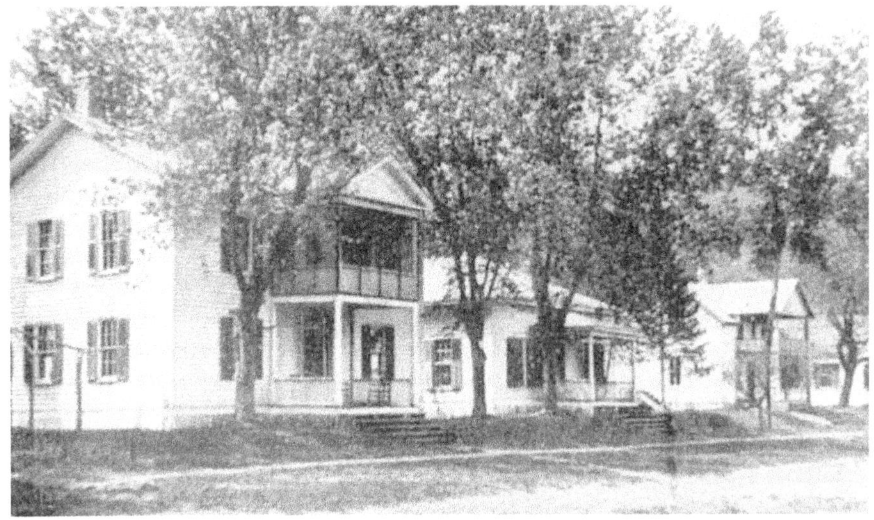

These cottages served generations of hotel guests and campers. *Flies Collection.*

lines. To make room for an attached garage, its next-door neighbor, Virginia, was razed. Grapevine was then put up for sale as a private residence. It was renamed the Kittle House, in memory of the family who originally built it in the 1860s.[87] Poplar, Pine and Fern will also probably be modernized in a similar fashion in the near future.

The Village

The village of Frontenac was laid out in 1857 as a rectangular grid on land lying just to the west of the terrace properties. While the original plat provided ample space for growth, most of those buildings built immediately preceding the Civil War, or shortly after it, tend to be clustered in the area north of McLean Street, between Manypenny Avenue and LeRoy Avenue. Street names are typically derived from the names of original settlers, with some exceptions. The original 1857 plan included a large park, named Vakondiota,[88] which divides the village from north to south. Shortly after the Civil War, Israel Garrard donated land on the southern edge of the village, near the intersection of Wood Avenue and Green Street, to serve as a cemetery. A narrow lane follows a ridge southward through Frontenac Cemetery, with family plots and individual graves of original settlers and their descendants on both sides. At its southernmost end is a circular drive surrounding the Garrard family burial plot.

The village today still has only one paved road, McLean Street, plus a short portion of Garrard Avenue, which is also County Road 2. The narrow graveled streets pass under large trees. The almost total absence of streetlights or utility poles contributes to a sense that one has entered a time machine and is again in a small New England village of the 1850s, magically transported to the raw Minnesota frontier.

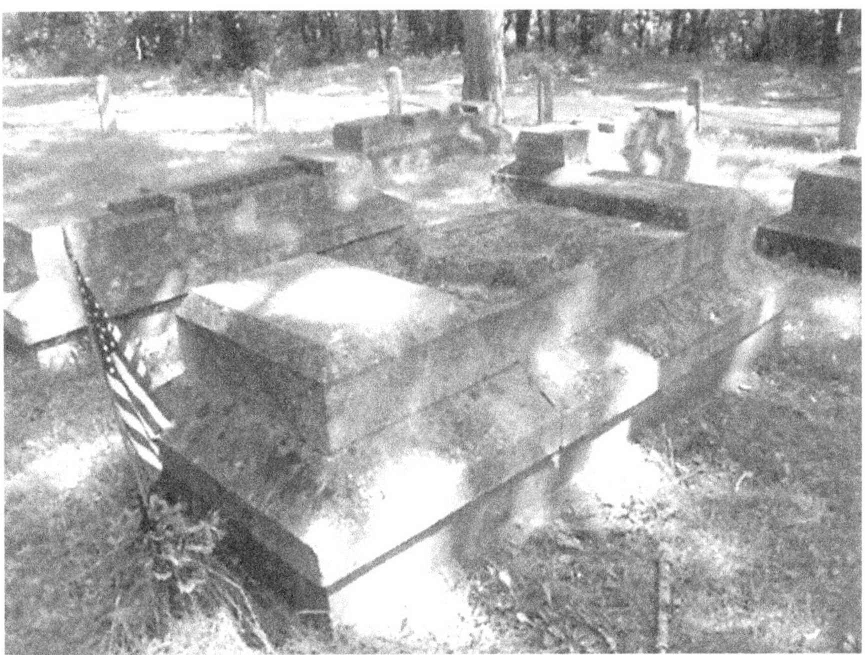

The Garrard family plot in Frontenac Cemetery.

Post Office, circa 1857

29039 Wood Avenue

This small structure served as Frontenac's first post office. The operation of a small rural post office was an important link in early communications, as settlement moved ever westward. The postmaster (or postmistress in many cases) received a small stipend from the federal government. In return, he would handle outgoing letters and parcels and hold incoming mail for pick up by recipients. In the earliest days, mail traveled exclusively by steamboat, but with the completion of the military road between Fort Snelling and Wabasha, regular service was ensured even during the winter months.

The building was also a private home and housed the postmaster's family. When Schneider's Tavern, just a block to the north, was established, it became a natural focus and meeting place for the village. The post office was moved there, probably in the late 1860s.

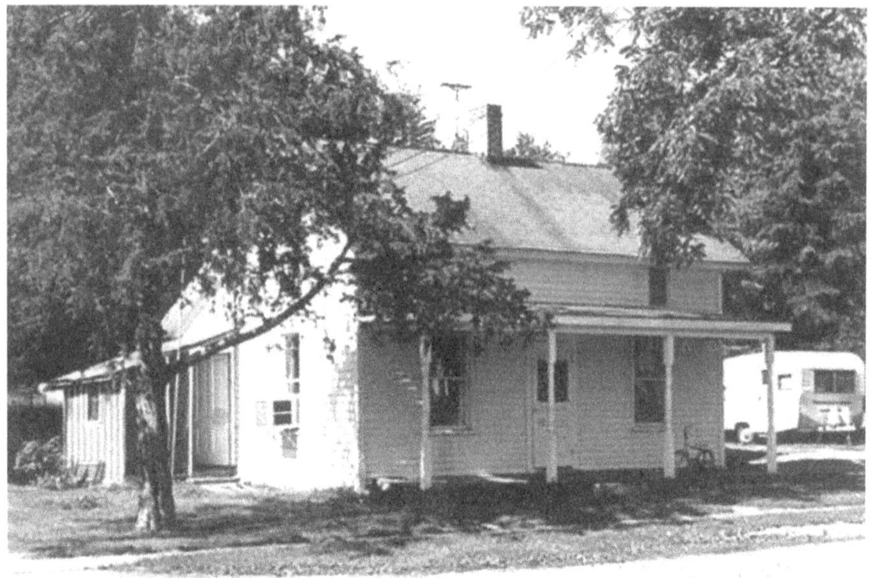

The original Frontenac Post Office, as it appeared in 1974. *Flies Collection.*

FRONTENAC SCHOOL, 1857

29659 County 2 Boulevard

The availability of a public school education to every child was a uniquely important factor in American history. Thus, it was one of the first concerns of the families arriving in the newly founded village of Frontenac. Officially known as Florence Township District 24, Frontenac School was erected on land donated by Israel Garrard, a raised knoll north of the current County Road 2 west of the village.[89] It served generations of local children in grades one through eight for ninety-seven years. In 1955, Goodhue County schools were consolidated, and the school was closed.[90]

The building reflects the typical one-room school so common across rural Minnesota until the middle of the twentieth century. Simple sash occupy the sidewalls, with their clapboard siding and vertical corner boards. A few additional touches of local craftsmanship exhibit the builders' pride in their school. The double entrance doors sport transoms to allow for light and ventilation. A wide front porch with steps along the full width evokes a memory of the prints of so many small feet over the years. And the elaborate, enclosed belfry, with its louvered openings, serves as a unique accent to the little school.

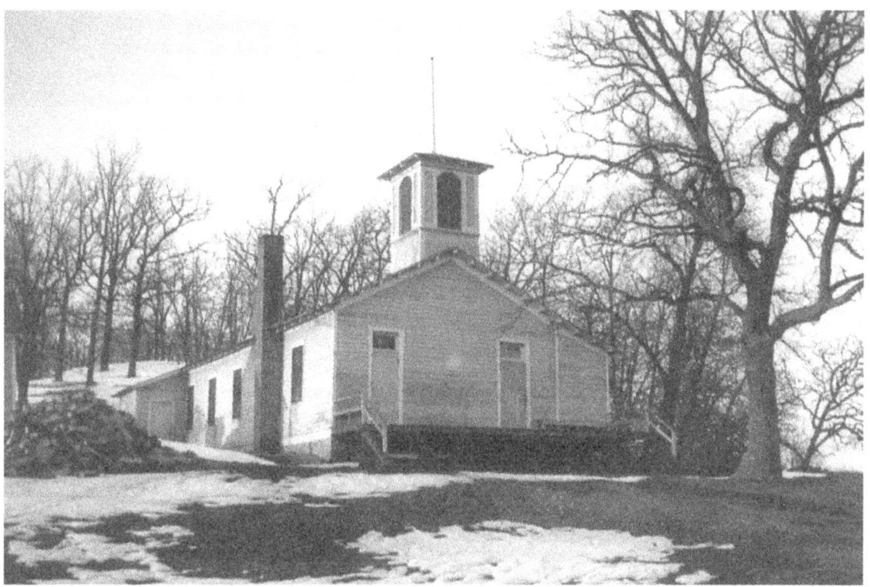

Frontenac School, taken in the 1950s near the end of a century of service. *Friends Collection.*

Henry Hunecke House, circa 1858

34962 Dakota Street

Shortly after his arrival in Frontenac, master builder Henry Hunecke acquired land from Israel Garrard and built this small house to serve as a home for his family. The enterprising Hunecke clan became a key part of village life. Keeping bees on the property, they provided honey to the village and hotel for many years, earning the house the nickname of "Honeybee Cottage,"[91] still used today. Another major source of income was the raising of chickens, thousands of which were used by the hotel in the preparation of its famous chicken dinners.[92] Henry's son, Ed Hunecke, in later years inherited his father's role as a leader in village affairs.

The house itself exhibits none of the extraneous details of some of the other structures near it. The practical German sensibilities of Henry Hunecke probably dictated a purely functional design for his own home. A two-story block faces north, with an unadorned main entrance. The single-story wing to the south has a porch on its east side. The arched trim on the porch, evocative of similar features on Winona Cottage, may have been a later addition. Though plain in appearance, this lovingly maintained little house, with its charming white picket fence, remains a key structure in the old village.

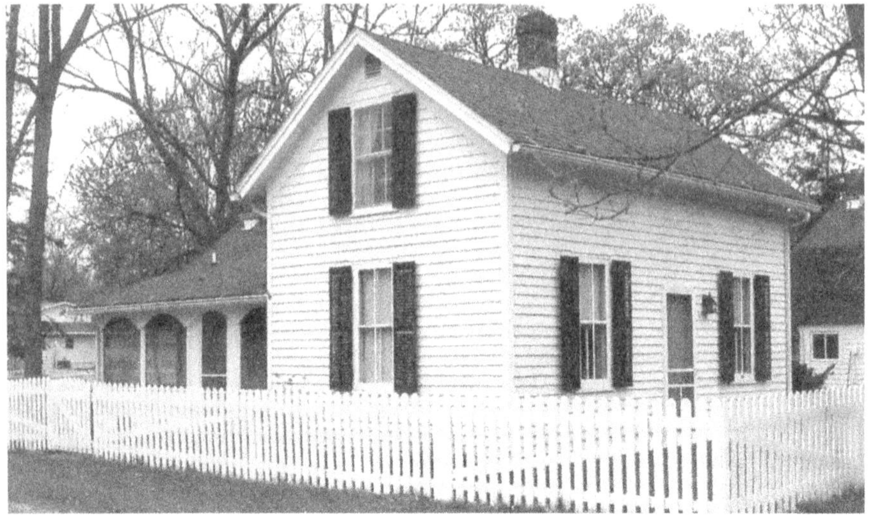

The Hunecke House. *Flies Collection.*

Little Dacotah, 1859 (Moved to current site in 1923)

34921 Dacotah Street

This small house originally was a wing on the north side of Dacotah Cottage. Part of the initial construction by Lewis Garrard in 1859, it housed his office plus some other rooms. An aerial photo of the village, taken from atop Garrard's Bluff in the 1880s, shows the wing attached to Dacotah Cottage. Its footprint and gable configuration match this house. Lewis Garrard was a medical doctor but never seriously pursued it as a career. His practice was limited to a few of the earliest settlers in Frontenac, plus the remaining Native Americans in the area. It was in this wing of the house that he saw his patients.

Ben and Florence Strupe were married in 1923. She came to Frontenac in 1921 to work as a nanny for a grandson[93] of George Wood Garrard. After the wedding, a wing of Dacotah Cottage was moved to this site and remodeled into a home for the newlywed couple. The result was dubbed "Little Dacotah" and still bears that nickname today. Mrs. Strupe remained in the house until her death in 1995. Serving as a bridge between original settlers and current residents, she became the unofficial matriarch of Old Frontenac, recounting the old stories and history of its people and buildings. She was a guiding force in preservationist efforts[94] during her entire life.

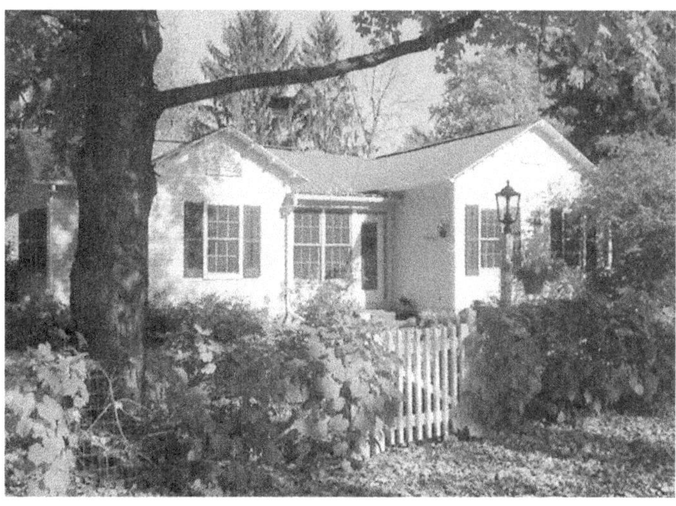

Little Dacotah.

The house still exhibits its lineage in its exposed rafters and twelve-paned windows. The footprint and layout of its gables match an archival photo of the northwest wing of Dacotah Cottage, though it was rotated ninety degrees from its original orientation when moved to this site. The clapboard siding and corner boards survive but are no longer the original white color always preferred by Mrs. Strupe. Subsequent owners have repainted the house, and it is now a soft yellow.

Schneider Tavern, 1862

28971 Wood Avenue

This structure was built by partners Engelbert Haller and Kasper Koch, with a loan from Israel Garrard. Their original intent was to operate it as a general store, but soon after its completion it was sold to a Mr. Schneider, who renamed it. The main floor served as a combination store and tavern, with one corner dedicated to the village post office. Travelers along the nearby military road, seeking simpler accommodations than the Lakeside Hotel, rented sleeping quarters on the second floor. Two separate entrances, on the east and south sides, allowed customers to access the store and post office without passing through the tavern area.

The building served as a social center for the small village for a number of years. It then became the private home of the son of Evert Westervelt. It was probably during his tenure as owner that the elaborate bay window on

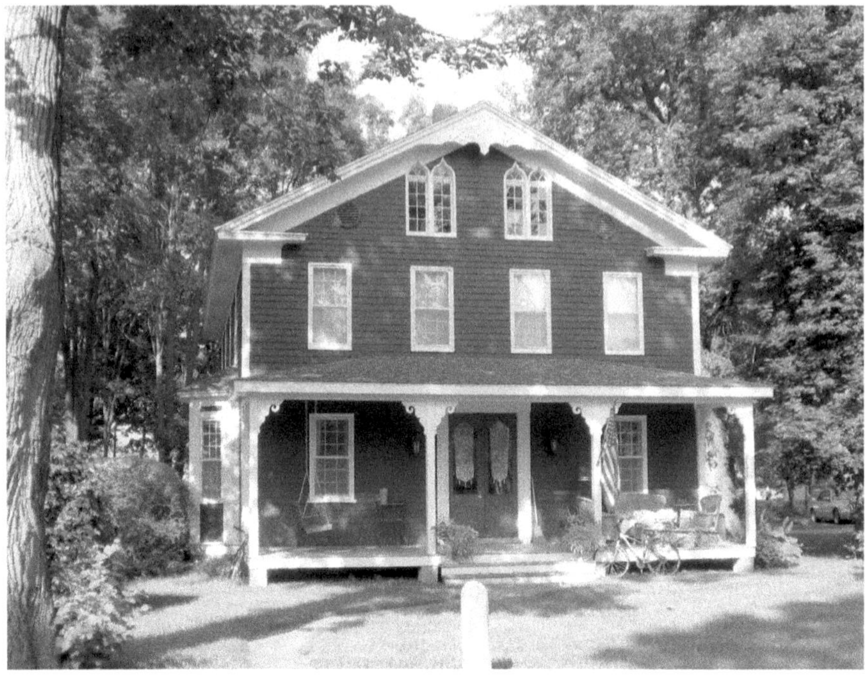

The Schneider Tavern, now a private residence.

the south side was added. By the 1970s, the old building was in marginal condition, but it was rescued and restored by subsequent and current owners. A 1980 photo shows the first stage of restoration, with a new, smaller porch topped by a Greek portico supported by square Doric columns. An elaborate scroll sawn detail has been added to the front gable end. Later restoration has returned the front porch to its larger, original configuration, but with more scroll details at the column heads. A unique feature of the house is the pair of doubled windows at the attic level, with their almost Moorish arched tops. It is not known if these are original to the building or were added later.

Louis Carlson House, circa 1867

28960 Wood Avenue

Originally built by Engelbert Haller, this house was soon acquired by Louis Carlson and is still owned by one of his descendants. Carlson was employed by Israel Garrard as a valet, but his duties transcended those of a mere body

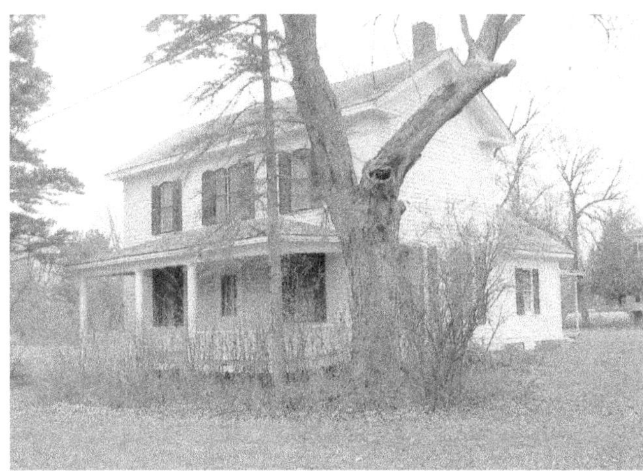

The Carlson House.
Friends Collection.

servant. His role at St. Hubert's Lodge was more that of chief steward, in charge of all the other servants and household finances, a true second in command to the old general.

The house exhibits typical Greek Revival features and, like Locust Lodge, is a fine example of that style. The main block is two stories high. Arched, recessed windows are of the six over six style and are flanked by matching shutters. Corner pilasters serve as vertical delimiters to the white clapboard siding. The roof's gable ends exhibit returns, which form a broken pediment. A deep gallery crosses the front, topped by a low hipped roof supported by four Doric columns. The one-story wing to the rear probably was added shortly after Carlson acquired the house.

Will Lubeck House, circa 1880 (Moved to current site in 1958)

28891 Manypenny Avenue

Originally the top story of the rearmost wing of Winona Cottage just to the east, this structure was salvaged during a remodeling project in 1958. It was moved to its current site, carefully raised and hoisted over the stone wall at the rear of the Winona Cottage property. After placement on a basement already prepared for it, the structure was remodeled into a private residence. Will and Min Lubeck, both descendants of original Frontenac settlers, moved into this small home. Mr. Lubeck, a talented carpenter,[95] performed the required remodeling.

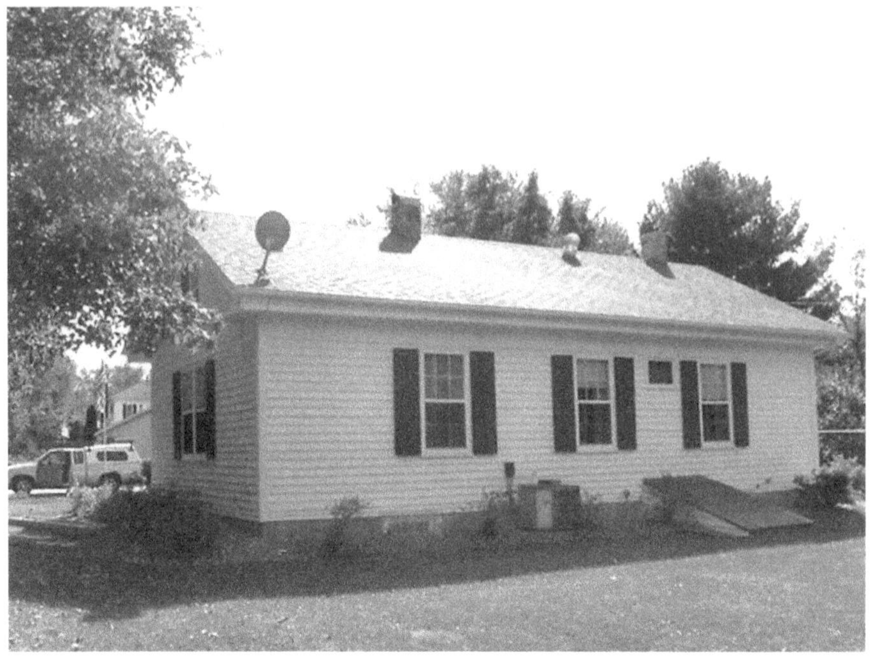

The Lubeck House.

The house still has the original sash on three sides, with the broken pediment at the roof returns typical of Winona Cottage. The west end was originally the open end connecting the wing to Winona Cottage. Mr. Lubeck carefully duplicated the siding, sash style and roof details at this end of his house, maintaining a simple Greek Revival appearance. The original structure was approximately twenty-two by twenty-two feet but was enlarged to provide more living space for the Lubecks.

Churches

When the first residents came to the new town of Frontenac in the 1850s, they brought their religion with them. At one period, three different Protestant churches coexisted in the village. Only one remains today. Israel Garrard was not a religious man and rarely attended services in any of the village churches, but by generous donations of land and money, he supported all of them, considering them to be a key part of the social fabric of Frontenac.

Campbellite Church, 1867 (Burned circa 1900)

(Northwest corner of McLean Street and Manypenny Avenue)

This church and its attendant parsonage were funded by Sarah Bella McLean shortly after her arrival to take up residence in 1862. A devout member of this fundamentalist sect, she wished to establish its presence in her new home. A number of early families in the area formed the new congregation. No photographs survive showing the actual church building in detail. However, a panoramic photo showing the entire village from atop Garrard's Bluff, taken in the 1880s, shows some features of the building. It was oriented with its entrance facing eastward and appears to be of a size similar to Christ Episcopal Church, its contemporary farther to the west along McLean Street. A tall bell tower rose from the entry foyer, topped by a low hipped roof. All construction was of wood.

When Mrs. McLean returned to Cincinnati in about 1880, the Campbellite congregation began to drift away to other denominations. Over the next

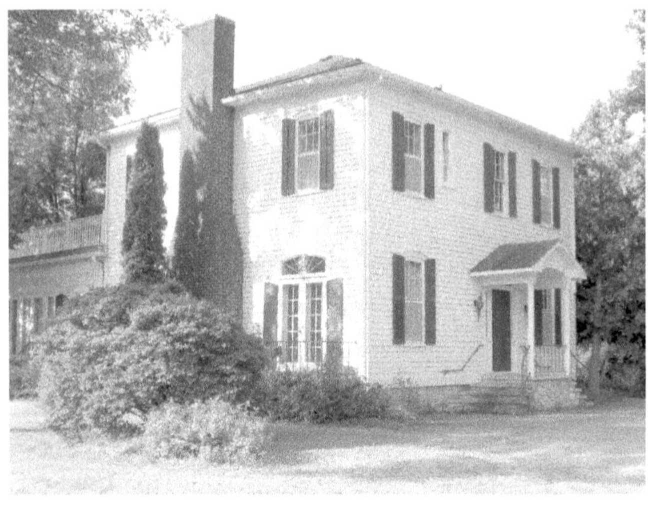

The parsonage for the Campbellite Church, now a private residence.

twenty years, the church was used by both Methodists and Baptists as a house of worship. Finally, in about 1900, lightning struck the bell tower, and the entire building was destroyed in the resulting fire.

The parsonage, built just to the north of the church, exhibits many of the Greek Revival decorative touches common to Frontenac buildings of the period. Large six-by-six double-hung windows are recessed in openings topped by a low arch. Curved top shutters fit snugly into these openings. The main entrance is reached via a small stone porch with steps on each side, topped by an arched roof with simple columns. Of particular interest is the stone porch on the east side of the house, reached via French doors and topped by a fanlight window. A low, pyramidal hipped roof tops the structure. A later one-story addition to the south is topped by a flat roof surrounded by a railing.

When the church was destroyed, the parsonage was vacated and sold to a private party. It was converted into a restaurant, the Moccasin Inn, which operated in the building until sometime after World War II. It then became a private residence.

CHRIST EPISCOPAL CHURCH, 1868

34661 Cathcart Street

When Nathaniel McLean arrived after the Civil War, he soon acquired a plot of land on the south side of McLean Street, across from his farm properties. On this site, he would erect Christ Episcopal Church and would serve as its lay

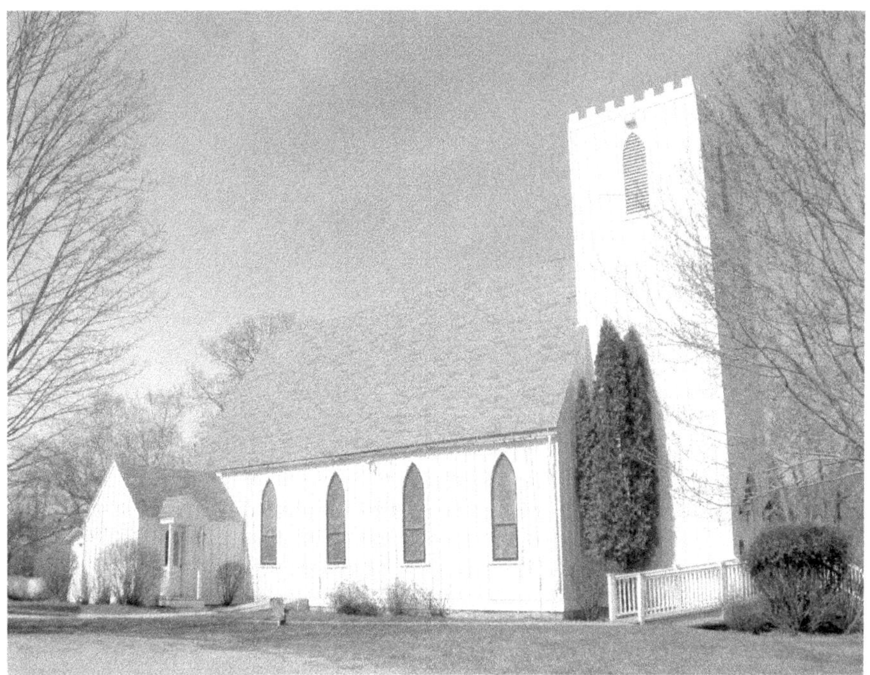

Christ Episcopal Church.

reader during his time in Frontenac. The church is built in the Gothic Revival style popularized by Richard Upjohn, a prominent eastern architect. In 1852, he published a plan book entitled *Rural Architecture*,[96] which featured a number of small Gothic churches. The design of Christ Church was probably heavily influenced by this book or drawn directly from it.

The construction exhibits Upjohn's typical vertical board and batten exterior, extending to the simple, crenelated bell tower over the entrance. All openings are arched in the Gothic style, all in fairly plain glass except for a stained grouping at the west end. The vertical boards and the site of the building on a low knoll give it a soaring appearance and disguise its actual small size. A small wing at the southeast corner was originally built as a sacristy, which now shares that space with modern amenities. The interior of the church is extremely open, with a high ceiling supported by simplified hammer beams. The building and its furnishings were all executed by master builder Henry Hunecke, whose grave is in the small cemetery behind the church.

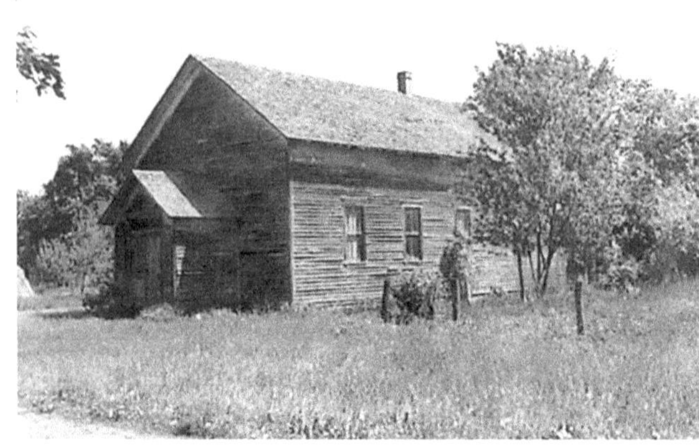

Norwegian Lutheran Church. *Friends Collection.*

GERMAN METHODIST CHURCH, 1873 (RAZED CIRCA 1950)

(Southeast corner of Wood Avenue and Faribault Street)

This church was initially built to house a small congregation of German settlers who had adopted the Methodist religion. Within a fairly short time, the congregation dwindled, and the building was purchased by a group with a different faith and a different national origin.

A number of early settlers in Frontenac were of Scandinavian origin and Lutheran as a result. When the congregation that would ultimately become St. John's Lutheran Church in Frontenac Station first formed in 1866, German Lutherans predominated. The relatively smaller group of Scandinavian Lutherans probably joined with their German brethren in the new congregation. When St. John's was built in 1871, it was under the auspices of a predominately German synod, and the Scandinavians withdrew to create a separate congregation with allegiance to a different synod.[97] The little church in Frontenac housed its second owner, known as the Norwegian Lutheran Church.

The building was a simple, unadorned structure. Sided with whitewashed clapboard, its one entrance was housed in a small vestibule on the west side. Windows were plain double-hung sash with minimal trim. Beside its much grander sister church, St. Johns, it pales by comparison and must have served a much smaller congregation. Unfortunately, no church records have survived to tell us more about the small group of families who worshiped in this little building. The congregation dissolved sometime before World War II, and by the late 1940s, the building was serving as a private dwelling. Sometime around 1950, it was finally vacated and torn down.

The Long Point Area

The fertile bottomland in the Frontenac area receives its water from a number of small streams rising in the bluffs to the west. These come together and form Wells Creek. Where the creek joins the Mississippi River, it has gradually, over thousands of years, deposited its burden of sand and silt to form a low point thrusting out into the river. Known by the French as Pont du Sable (Sand Point) and by later settlers as Long Point, it housed the first white settlement in the area and also its first Christian church. The point is now part of Frontenac State Park and is a nature preserve. A hiking trail allows one to walk to the end of the point and enjoy a view of Lake Pepin.

Old French Forts, 1727, 1731 and 1750

When the Sieur de Perrier led his party of French traders ashore on the beach of Pont au Sable (now Long Point) in 1727, they immediately set to work. Well armed and experienced, their first priority was to build a fort to protect themselves and their goods. The size of the total party is unknown, but general documentation about the French fur trade would indicate about ten to fifteen men, including the two Jesuit priests who accompanied the party. They quickly laid out and constructed a fort along the lines of a proven and somewhat standardized plan, used in countless frontier trading operations. The new fort was named Fort Beauharnois for the French governor general of Canada.

A square stockade of sharpened logs sunk in the earth was erected first, with one strong gate, and all goods moved inside for safekeeping. Two raised, unroofed bastions were built at opposite corners of the stockade, allowing defenders a field of fire along all four walls. The usual dimensions of the stockade would be approximately one hundred feet on a side, with a stockade height of eight to ten feet. Only after the stockade was completed did the party start to construct the simple shelters within that would allow them to winter over and be ready for the spring trading sessions with the native people of the region. An indeterminate number of huts, probably three or four, were built within the stockade. They were freestanding, allowing quick passage of defenders inside the stockade walls. Construction was of the "Poteaux en terre" method,[98] similar to the stockade with vertical logs placed in the earth. Openings were minimal to preserve warmth, with a door to shut out the wind and cold. Each hut had a fire pit below a crude wattle and daub chimney. The structures were roofed with rough bark, weighted down with rocks.

One of these huts was allocated to a small chapel for the use of the two Jesuits in saying their obligatory daily masses. They dedicated it to Saint Michael the Archangel, and it is acknowledged by historians to be the first church in the state of Minnesota. The purpose of having priests accompanying every trading party was to bring the Roman Catholic religion to the native people. No record exists regarding their level of success in this instance.

But the primary business of the party was trade. Concerned by the proximity to the massive river and the threat of high water, the Sieur de Perriere was reassured by the local natives that flooding was not a problem and built near the beach.[99] After two straight years of inundations in the spring, the fort was destroyed by the traders, who then departed downriver. But trade had been so good that in 1731 that a second party, under the Sieur de Linctot, returned to Pont au Sable and rebuilt Fort Beauharnois on the same plan, but on higher ground.[100]

This second fort lasted until 1737, when intertribal warfare made trade impossible. After burning the stockade and buildings, the traders again withdrew from the area. Another party returned and rebuilt yet again in 1750, remaining until all French Canadian trading operations ceased in 1757 after the French and Indian War. Fort Beauharnois was the last French post in Minnesota.

KINGSLEY MILL, 1876 (RAZED CIRCA 1940)

(On Long Point, near County Road 2)

The Wells Creek watershed supported a number of small milling operations in the nineteenth century, taking advantage of the small creek and its tributaries to power their machinery. Only one of these is within the area covered by this book. In 1876, Fred Kingsley erected his mill along Wells Creek where

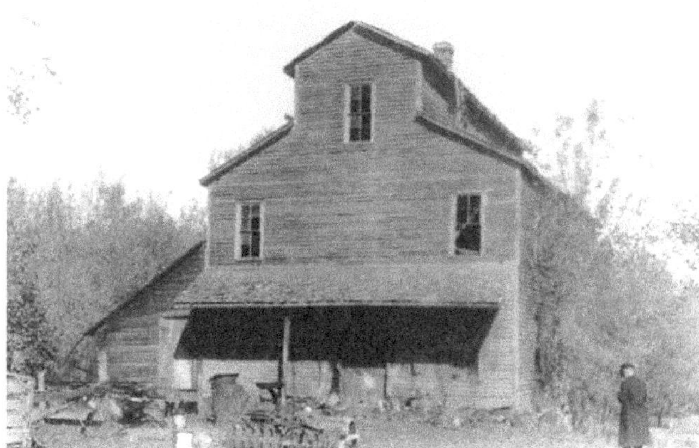

Kingsley Mill, taken in the 1930s. *Friends Collection.*

it entered Long Point and proceeded to carve its final course to the nearby Mississippi River. Because of the low rise of the creek and the flat terrain, the mill probably featured an undershot wheel. Generating less horsepower than the more traditional overshot style,[101] it had the advantage of not requiring construction of a dam to form a millpond. Instead, a simple ditch called a sluice diverted the creek's water under the structure to power the wheel.

The milling process was based not only on water power but also on gravity. Arriving grain was hoisted to the top floor by screw elevators. It then passed through a series of grinding millstones as it made its way to the lowest level, where the end product was collected and bagged. The mill building existed well into the twentieth century but probably stopped operations earlier. Access to the railroad at Frontenac Station gave farmers the option of shipping their grain directly to other, more efficient mills like those in Minneapolis and other area towns, such as Red Wing and Lake City. The building, surrounded by remnants of its rusting machinery, stood until about 1940, when it was finally torn down. Nothing remains of the original sluice or the building, except for a few foundation stones.[102]

Villa Maria, 1891 (Burned 1969)

29847 County 2 Boulevard

After Israel Garrard donated 124 acres of his land in 1885 to build a new school, the Ursuline nuns in Lake City began to muster their resources to build on the property. The site is elevated slightly above Long Point and proceeds in

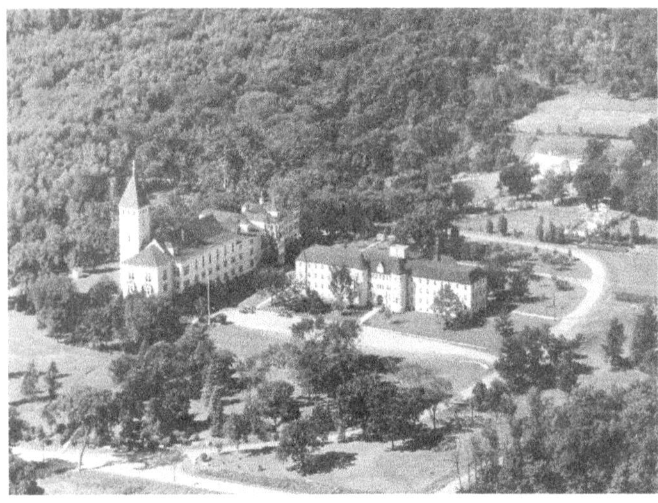

Villa Maria, with the original 1891 building to the left. *Friends Collection.*

a generally westerly direction from the base of the point. The second and third French forts had occupied this site only 130 years before. A site was chosen for the new building well up the slope, safe from flooding. Benefactors well known to Mother Ligouri were solicited, and funds were pledged to cover the cost of the new private school for girls, to be named Villa Maria.

In 1888, a set of plans was executed by F.F. Evans, an architect from St. Louis.[103] Construction commenced in 1889, and the building was completed in 1891. A large number of skilled workmen were required to build such a large project, and many were drawn from the region. Among these was a large contingent of Frontenac men, led by Henry Hunecke. Israel Garrard was highly interested in the project and monitored its progress on his frequent visits[104] to the site. Even though the construction crew was not exclusively from Frontenac, the local men felt a special affinity for this important addition to their small settlement on Lake Pepin. The dedication was held on September 8, 1891, and was a gala affair[105] with fifteen hundred people in attendance. Archbishop Ireland of St. Paul officiated, assisted by Bishop Cotter of the Winona Diocese. Israel Garrard attended and was lauded for his generosity.

The building, when finished, was four stories in height over a full basement. Construction was of wood. A tall bell tower on the south side of the structure contained a large arched window over the main entrance to the chapel inside. On the south side was a large wing, also four stories in height. Classrooms and dining facilities occupied the main floor, with the upper floors allocated to living quarters for students and the nuns. On the exterior, the first and second floors featured groups of paired double-hung windows, while those on the

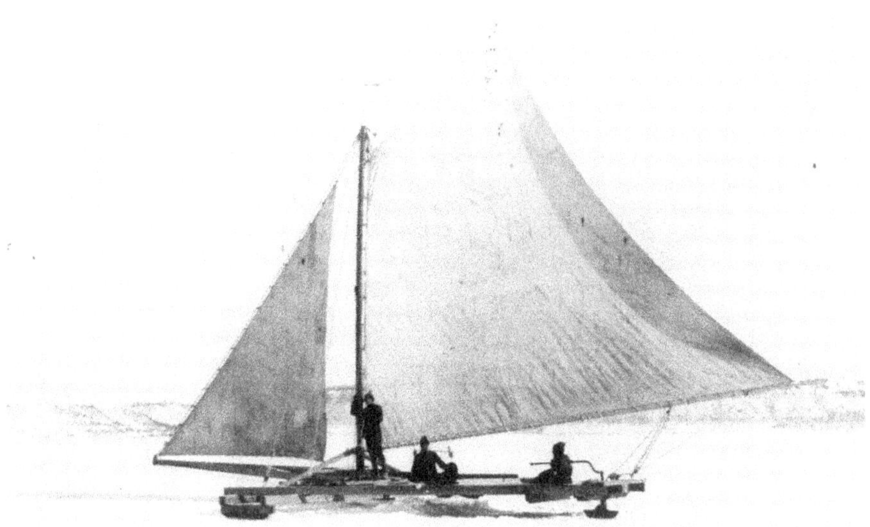

Villa Maria students crew the *Admiral Byrd*, the school's iceboat. *Friends Collection.*

third were single windows with arched tops. The fourth, the attic level, had a number of small dormer windows.

Villa Maria operated as a boarding school for young women until about 1970. Its population varied, but at its peak times it was approximately 130 girls plus 25 nuns and other staff. In 1946, Walter Butler & Company of Minneapolis was commissioned to design and build a second building. It was connected to the 1891 building by a pedestrian tunnel. This structure, named Marian Hall, is the current Villa Maria. In the early 1960s, a third, smaller structure was added to house a swimming pool between the two larger buildings. On March 20, 1969, in the early morning hours, lightning struck the bell tower of the 1891 building and started a fire that, within four hours, reduced the old school to a pile of ashes. A strong north wind fanned the flames but also served to spare Marian Hall and the pool building, situated immediately to the north. All students were safely evacuated, and no life was lost.

After the fire, the Ursulines determined that it was not feasible to rebuild, and a decision was made to close the school. The remaining buildings became a retreat and convention center. In 1998, a new convention center, Ursuline Hall, was built on the site of the original 1891 building.

Frontenac Station

Before 1873 and the coming of the railroad, there was no real town at the junction of the north–south Military Road and the single road to Frontenac, two miles away on the river. In 1871, a new church was built to take advantage of the access to these roads. After 1873, a thriving community quickly grew up near the newly laid tracks. The original plat consisted of eight square blocks with street names evoking the nations of the world: Germania, Italia, Britannia, Hibernia and Scandinavia. The sole exception to the convention was Ludlow Avenue, named for the maternal branch of the Garrard family. Honoring America, the name Columbia was reserved for the main street across the tracks from the depot. Businesses were soon established along the east side of Columbia Street, joined by a new Florence Town Hall. Though the eventual demise of rail traffic curtailed much of its activity, the town remains a viable community, with many of its residents commuting to jobs in other locales. U.S. Highway 61 now follows Columbia Street.

St. John's Lutheran Church, 1871

33685 Germania Street

This building predates the founding of Frontenac Station by two years. The congregation, made up of German-speaking Lutheran settlers from the area, was founded in 1866, with the church being erected five years later. The church is still very active and is associated with the Wisconsin Synod of the Lutheran Church.

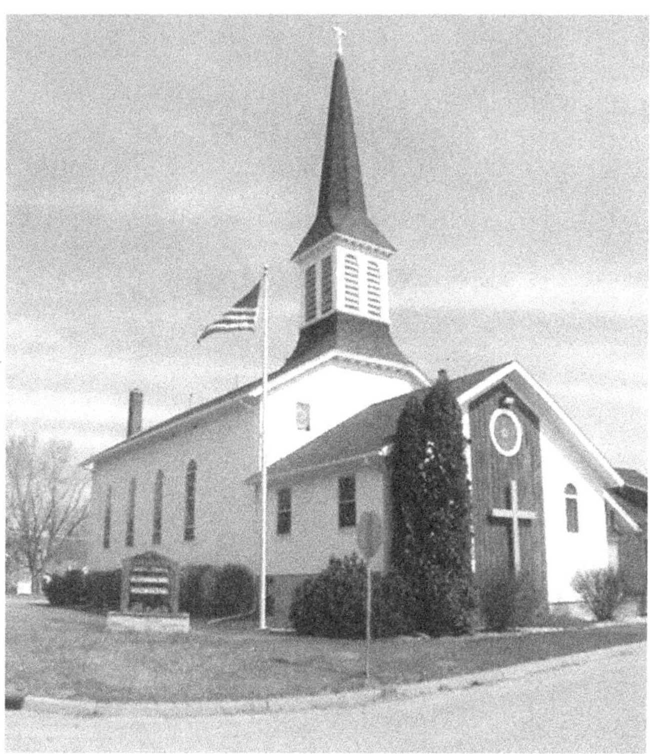

St. John's Lutheran Church.

The original white clapboard church, with its tall arched windows, rests on a raised basement constructed of local limestone. It was augmented in 1895 by a bell tower on the west end. The tower had a mansard base supporting the main bell chamber, topped by a handsome spire. An oval window fronted the lower tower, above an arched entry door. Wide stone steps led to the entrance. In 1977, a large entry wing was added in front of the tower, which now masks the original detail of the facade.

Depot, circa 1875 (Razed circa 1960)

West side of Railroad Tracks, across from the Town Hall

As the railroad was constructed in 1873 between LaCrosse and St. Paul, temporary structures were thrown up along the right of way to serve as depots for the many customers anxious to utilize the new services. Often these were nothing more than worn-out boxcars, stripped of their trucks, with a

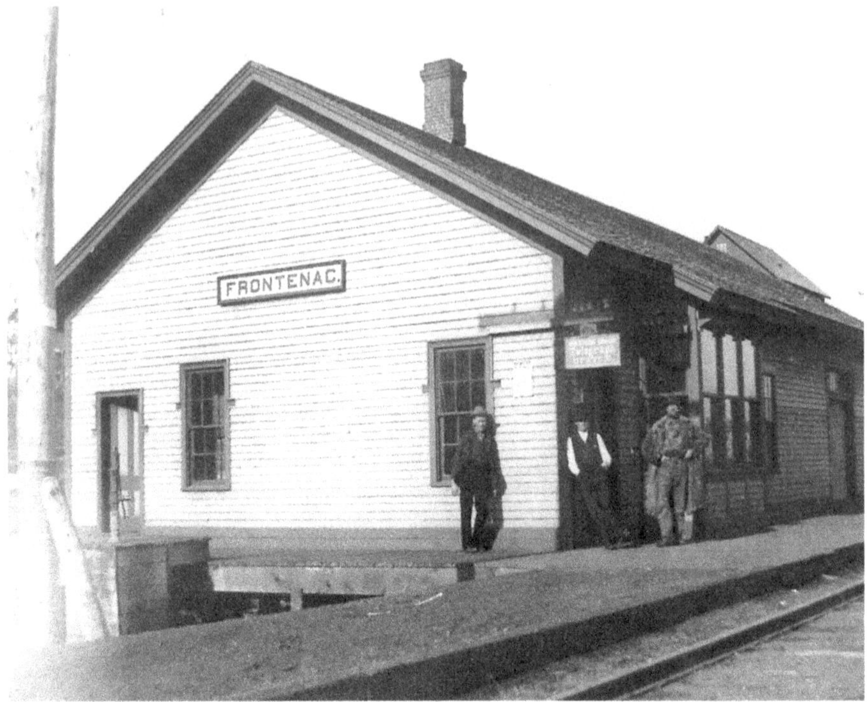

Depot. *Friends Collection.*

rough platform. Within a few years, crews of Milwaukee Road carpenters had replaced these temporary structures with new depots. Created from a selection of standard plans, the depots varied from small, unmanned way stations, where unscheduled stops were made to pick up or deliver goods, to those elaborate stations reserved for major junctions[106] with other railroads. Between these two extremes was a standard design, intended for placement at scheduled stops to handle both freight and passengers. Because of the volume of freight expected and the number of passengers arriving or departing from the Lakeside Hotel, Frontenac Station received one of these depots, and the Milwaukee Road added it to its master timetable of scheduled stops.

The building was of sturdy wood construction, with clapboard siding and simple double-hung windows. Two entrances opened onto a tamped gravel platform area. At the south end was an entrance to the passenger waiting room, ticketing area and office. At the north end was a larger door accessing the freight and baggage handling area. Between these was a bay with large windows on three sides, allowing the stationmaster to observe passing traffic. In daytime, the depot was staffed by a crew of at least three: stationmaster, telegrapher and freight handler. A lone telegrapher manned the depot at night, his lamp probably the only light in the tiny town.

A large grain elevator was erected to the north of the depot. This structure, served by its own siding, was separately staffed and handled storage and shipment of grain from area farms. Operated by the Van Dusen firm,[107] it served to feed the ever more demanding appetite for grain at Twin Cities flour mills. After World War II ended, the railroad business dwindled. By 1950, passenger service had been totally eroded by competition from private automobiles, and large trucks transported the majority of the local produce. Trains no longer stopped at Frontenac Station. The old depot had finally outlived its usefulness and was torn down.

Florence Town Hall, 1875

33923 Columbia Street (U.S. Highway 61)

This structure, built on land donated by Israel Garrard, is a survivor. Erected as a government center for Florence Township, this building also served as a social center for local events and entertainments. It has always functioned as a community center and a focus of civic pride. It is the oldest town hall in Minnesota, continuously filling that role for almost one and a half centuries. The original building of 1875 was only thirty-four by forty-six feet, with one main room. In 1916, it was extended to the rear by another twenty-two feet. The addition housed an elevated stage with dressing facilities and toilet. A later expansion added a kitchen area. A sheltered entrance faces Columbia Street; an oval above the entrance proudly displays "1875," the year of its construction. The exteriors of the original hall and the stage addition are clad in drop siding, while clapboards cover the more recent kitchen addition. Windows in the hall are tall, with arches and hoods. Above them, the low pitched roof is supported by paired brackets, spaced along the eaves. The sheltered entrance has been pierced to accommodate a ramp for handicapped access, a recent addition to the building.

In 1995, a number of Frontenac Station residents felt that the old hall had outlived its usefulness and proposed the construction of a modern replacement. A battle ensued to save the old building, spearheaded by the Friends of Florence Town Hall, an active local preservation group. With support from the Minnesota Historical Society and other interested parties, a case was made for the restoration and continued use of the venerable structure.

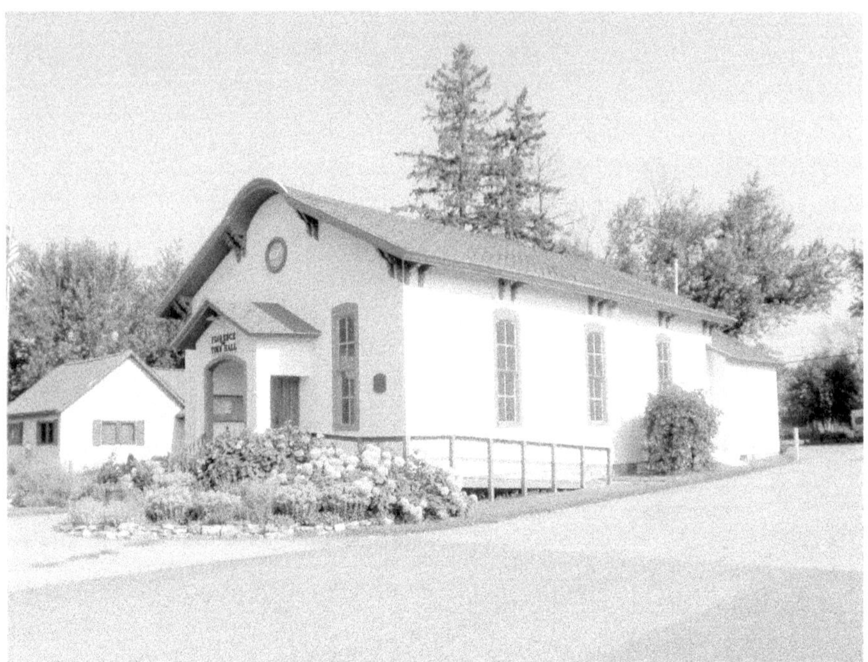

Florence Town Hall.

A referendum was put before township voters, and the building was saved. After restoration, the building was added to the National Register of Historic Places in 2000. In addition to its continuing role in township government, the building now contains the archives of the Friends of Florence Township, plus a display of historic photos and artifacts.

Notes

The Land (Before 1853)

1. The first documented mention of the point occurs in Father Louis Hennepin's account of his journey in 1680 up the river to the great falls he named after St. Anthony, now the site of Minneapolis. While encamped on Pont au Sable, his party encountered a Dakota war party returning from a raid to the south. Observing the great mourning by the warriors for one of their fallen comrades, Hennepin dubbed Lake Pepin the *Lac de Pleurs* ("Lake of Tears").
2. The name is also sometimes rendered as "Lakota," but the Dakota name is almost universally used today by scholars and also in tribal publications. In Minnesota, the Dakota were loosely divided into four bands: Mdewakenton, Wapekute, Wahpeton and Sisseton. To the western Dakota of South Dakota and Wyoming, these eastern bands were lumped together under the name of "Santee." It was primarily the Mdewakenton Dakota who populated the banks of the Mississippi River where our story takes place. The variation "Dacotah" is used in Frontenac place names, so I have tried to consistently use it only to refer to those, while "Dakota" is reserved for Native American references.
3. Most sources date the first appearance of the Dakota on the west bank of the Mississippi River to about AD 1500.
4. Prairie Island today is a reservation of the Mdewakenton band of the Dakota.
5. The treaty created the Northwest Territory, from which five states were eventually formed: Ohio in 1803, Indiana in 1816, Illinois in 1818, Michigan in 1837 and Wisconsin in 1848.

6. Originally, the fort was known as Fort Saint Anthony for the nearby falls of the same name. Upon its completion in 1825, it was renamed in honor of its first commander, Josiah Snelling. Overseeing the construction performed by his regiment, the Fifth United States Infantry, Colonel Snelling suffered continuing bouts of dysentery. His poor health finally caused his recall to Washington in 1827, and he died a year later. One can still visit the fort, now fully restored to its 1820s appearance, and greet Colonel Snelling in the person of a reenactor, plus other residents of the old military post.
7. Steamboats first appeared on the lower Mississippi River in about 1812 and soon became common sights, carrying freight and passengers between St. Louis and New Orleans. The upper river presented difficulties in terms of rapids, so it was not until 1823 that the steamboat *Virginia* first arrived at the foot of St. Anthony's Falls, today the site of Minneapolis. Not until the twentieth century would the upper river be tamed by a series of locks and dams, making possible the busy barge traffic seen today.
8. In the Dakota language, the word means "fountain" or "spring."
9. Alexander was the son of Jean Baptiste Faribault, a highly successful early trader. His restored trading post can be visited today in Mendota, Minnesota. Alexander founded the town of Faribault on the Cannon River. His home there, owned by the Rice County Historical Society, can also be visited.
10. Wabasha (or Wapahasha II) was a major leader of the Dakota along the western shore of the Mississippi River, establishing a seasonal trading camp on the site of the town that still bears his name. In 1830, his indebtedness to white traders probably was what induced him to surrender tribal lands to form the half-breed tracts. There were actually three leaders of this name. Wapahasha I (1718–1806), also called "Red Cap," sided with the British in the American Revolution. Wapahasha II (1760–1836), known as Le Feuille ("the Feather") allied with Tecumseh and the British in the War of 1812. He signed a number of treaties with the government. Wapahasha III (1812–1876), also called Tatespin ("Bounding Wind" in Dakota) participated in the great uprising in 1862 and was present at the siege of New Ulm, Minnesota.
11. The issuance of the scrip gave rise to a great deal of land speculation in the Minnesota Territory, and tracts were bought up at bargain prices, sometimes as little as twenty-five cents per acre. The price paid by Evert Westervelt and Israel Garrard for the tracts held by Jane Wells and her sister, Elizabeth Faribault, are not recorded. However, due to the prominence of their husbands in the territorial legislature, one can assume that a fair price was offered and accepted in 1853. In the aftermath of the uprising in 1862, predatory speculators gobbled up remaining scrip from mixed-blood

Dakota, many of whom were imprisoned at Fort Snelling during the bitter winter months of 1862–1863. Notable in this action was Franklin Steele, an early land speculator who actually owned Fort Snelling and leased it back to the United States government during the Civil War years. A large quantity of prisoners' scrip would end up in Steele's hands in exchange for rations, favors or even release from the prison camp. For a fuller narrative regarding this, see "The Great Treasure of the Fort Snelling Prison Camp," in the *Minnesota History Quarterly* for Spring 2010.

ARRIVAL OF THE GARRARDS (1854–1860)

12. No real trace of Florence survives. It was located near the current Hansen's Harbor marina, north of Lake City.
13. An 1849 St. Paul newspaper account states that the best fistfighter in the Minnesota Territory was Territorial Governor Henry Sibley. As a close second, the account goes on to name Territorial Representative James "Bully" Wells. The events surrounding the territorial legislature and its deliberations must have been an interesting time.
14. When the uprising started, Wells and two of his sons were on their way west on a trading trip. To avoid the rampaging bands of Dakota, they swung south. Just across the Iowa border, they were captured by a war party, which prepared to put all three to death. Wells pointed out that his two sons had a Dakota mother and did not deserve to be killed. Bully was murdered, but the sons were spared and survived to tell the story of their father's bravery.
15. Jeptha Dudley Garrard (1802–1837) served two terms as the governor of Kentucky. He married Sarah Bella Ludlow in 1824. Ten years after his death, Sara Bella remarried.
16. Captain Nathaniel McLean was a brother of John McLean, Lewis's stepfather. He was uncle and namesake to the other Nathaniel McLean, who would ultimately join his stepbrothers in Frontenac.
17. Fort Union was a western outpost established by the United States Army in 1828 and in existence until 1867. It was situated on the upper Missouri River just west of the current city of Williston, North Dakota, on the border with Montana. The fort would have been an ideal site for the brothers to use as a center for their own exploration of the surrounding territory. It may still be visited today as a historic site maintained by the National Park Service.
18. Much of this story derives from a group of unpublished letters from Lewis to his mother, written during a brief period in September 1854. Transcribed

and preserved by a later resident of Greystone, they exhibit Lewis's growing frustration with the weather, his traveling companions and his missing brother.

19. There are a number of theories about how Israel Garrard chose this name and convinced his brothers to approve it. The most accepted is that Israel was honoring one of his ancestors, a French Huguenot refugee to the American colonies.
20. For a detailed history of this military road and a description of its route, see chapter 2 of *Tracing Minnesota's Old Government Roads*, a pamphlet issued by the Minnesota Historical Society in 1974.
21. Minnesota did not become a state until 1858.
22. Most of the old military road between Frontenac and Lake City still exists today as a township road. To find it, take County Road 2 west from Frontenac Station and cross the railroad tracks. You will find a gravel road that goes off to the left marked "Territorial Road." Following it will bring you back to County Road 5 just north of Lake City.
23. The details of Henry Hunecke's life are drawn from his obituary in the *Red Wing Daily Republican*, "Death of an Old Settler," dated December 2, 1907.
24. Between 1853 and 1939, a number of famous faces appeared among the guests at either St. Hubert's Lodge or at the nearby hotel. Among these were Henry Ward Beecher, Ulysses S. Grant, Harriet Beecher Stowe and Henry David Thoreau. James J. Hill and other notables from the Twin Cities would visit as they cruised the river in their elaborate yachts. Drs. William J. and Charles H. Mayo would stop by during their outings on Dr. Will's *Northstar* to enjoy a chicken dinner at the hotel. Author F. Scott Fitzgerald wrote of the many appealing young ladies he encountered during his visit.
25. Shortly after acquiring the land north of Frontenac point, Israel Garrard started quarrying the vein of fine dolomite along the front of Point No Point (later called Garrard's Bluff). This quarry had originally been opened by Evert Westervelt shortly after his arrival in 1853. Besides being used for foundations around the village, this fine-grained stone also was shipped east in great quantities. One of the most notable uses of the so-called Frontenac Stone arose from a visit in 1883 by two young tourists, architects Christopher LaFarge and George Heins. They would later specify the use of this stone in their Church of St. John the Divine in New York City. The quarry was managed by two members of the Carstenson family, Casper and John.
26. The trees for lumber were found on the neighboring bluffs. The flat terrace area itself was a sparsely wooded savannah when first settled. Israel

Garrard imported hardwoods from the bluffs and had them planted along the village streets. These streets are still shaded today by oak, elm and maple trees, plus other species.

SERVING THE UNION (1861–1865)

27. At age seventeen, Lewis Garrard was seeking adventure. He traveled to St. Louis and joined a company of traders sent west along the Santa Fe Trail, commanded by a Mr. St. Vrain, partner in the firm of Bent, St. Vrain & Co. Along the trail, the party saw extensive action with the Commanches around Fort Mann. Upon his return to Cincinnati, Lewis published his journal as a book, *Wah-To-Yah and the Taos Trail.* The book was one of a number of then-popular guidebooks purchased by potential pioneers preparing to travel west. Lewis later published a second book, *Chambersburg in the Colonies and Revolution*, a biography of his ancestor, General James Chambers.
28. John McLean was born in 1785 in New Jersey. As a boy, he moved with his parents to Virginia and Kentucky, finally settling in southern Ohio. Admitted to the Ohio bar in 1807, he practiced law until 1813, when he was elected to the U.S. House of Representatives, serving there until 1816. He was then appointed to the Supreme Court of Ohio, where he served until 1822. Between 1823 and 1829, he served as U.S. postmaster general under two presidents, James Monroe and John Quincy Adams. On March 17, 1829, President Andrew Jackson appointed him an associate justice of the Supreme Court of the United States. He would serve in that office until his death on April 3, 1861. Justice McLean was strongly in the antislavery camp. During his tenure on the Supreme Court, he would write a number of opinions opposing slavery, notably the minority opinion in the Dred Scott case. In the 1830s and 1840s, McLean was frequently mentioned as a potential Whig Party candidate for the presidency. He joined the new Republican Party in 1856 and narrowly lost the nomination to John C. Fremont. Again, in 1860, he was edged out by Abraham Lincoln. In 1807, he married Rebecca E. Edwards. After her death, he married Sarah Bella Ludlow Garrard in 1847.
29. General David Twiggs, commanding the Texas Department for the U.S. Army, turned over nineteen different forts and materiel depots to the provisional secessionist government even before Texas officially seceded from the Union on February 1, 1861. Twiggs's actions caused his discharge from the army in March 1861 on grounds of "treachery to the flag." All

army personnel in Texas were immediately taken into custody and gathered together at Austin. Some officers and enlisted men immediately enlisted in the new Confederate forces, and the remainder were paroled and released within a month.

30. This assignment may not have been as prestigious as it appears. By mid-1861, West Point was becoming something of a backwater posting. In June, the classes of 1861 and 1862 were both graduated and commissioned into the regular army due to a pressing need for officers. Many of the lower classmen resigned from the academy to accept volunteer commissions in units being raised by various states. Others resigned in 1861 to serve in the Confederate army. Thus the student body was continually shrinking during Kenner's brief tenure as commandant.
31. In January 1863, Lincoln's Emancipation Proclamation went into effect, freeing all slaves in the seceding states.
32. The idea of brevet promotions of higher rank in the regular army was a unique feature of the Civil War. A brevet promotion allowed regular army officers to serve temporarily at a higher rank until the end of the war, with the understanding that they would revert to their former rank at that time. One notable example was "General" George Armstrong Custer, brevetted a brigadier general in the Civil War. He reverted to the rank of lieutenant colonel in 1866 and still carried that rank when killed at Little Bighorn in 1876. The notion of brevet promotions was soon adopted for the volunteer units raised by individual states for Civil War service. As the war neared its end, many state governors rewarded volunteer officers with brevet promotions just prior to their mustering out, as a reward for their service and also for political purposes.
33. The famed Buffalo Soldiers actually consisted of two regiments of cavalry: the Tenth, mustered at St. Louis in May 1866, and the Ninth, mustered at New Orleans a few weeks later. Brigaded together but serving at widely separated locations, they established a tradition of excellence that continues today.

THE PASTORAL ESTATE (1866–1872)

34. In eastern newspapers dating from the 1870s and 1880s, Frontenac is often referred to as "the Newport of the West," a flattering comparison to that highly exclusive enclave of eastern wealth in Newport, Rhode Island.

35. The Garrards, primarily Israel but also his brothers, and Nathaniel McLean appear intermittently on many Frontenac abstracts throughout the last half of the nineteenth century. Sometimes they appear multiple times on one abstract usually for brief periods, giving rise to a local legend that the brothers liked to gamble and that they would use their various properties as stakes. The true reason is probably a bit more prosaic. Before banks started granting individual mortgages in the early twentieth century, private loans between individuals were negotiated to obtain lots and build structures on them. The Garrards financed virtually all such transactions in Frontenac but did not own the actual property. Instead, their names on the abstracts denoted temporary liens until the true owner repaid them.
36. Some sources erroneously state that Schneider's Tavern was the same building as the Pavilion, Evert Westervelt's original store and residence on the waterfront. These sources also state that Israel Garrard moved the Pavilion onto the site of the tavern in 1868 and had it remodeled. The Pavilion did indeed move in 1868, but it never left the waterfront. Moved back beyond the cart way, it functioned for many years as an outbuilding to the hotel. When the waterfront became a church camp in the 1940s, the building was renamed "Benjamin" and served as a craft center and auditorium. It survived until the 1990s, when it was finally razed.
37. Jeptha Garrard's farm, devoted primarily to the breeding and training of horses, was just to the north of County Road 2, across from Christ Episcopal Church.
38. Traces of this small track can still be found in the small wooded area just south of Christ Episcopal Church.
39. For a good description of navigation on the upper river in the 1870s, refer to Mark Twain's book *Life on the Mississippi*, where he tells in detail of a round trip between St. Louis and St. Paul.

TWO FRONTENACS (1873 TO PRESENT)

40. In the years following the Civil War, railroad mileage in the United States expanded at an incredible rate. Between 1866 and 1890, a significant amount of this expansion centered in the newly settled states immediately west of the Mississippi River. The main lines running from east to west across Minnesota bypassed many of the small settlements dependent on agriculture. Getting crops to market was the paramount concern for a small Minnesota town's survival. This, coupled with attendant civic pride

and boosterism, led many local businessmen to finance and build railroad lines to connect their town with the nearest main line. These short lines were typically purchased soon after their completion and absorbed into the main line's holdings. Profits were substantial for the initial local investors. This would result in a web of railroads across the southern half of Minnesota. Maps of the time show many short lines whose names are now just forgotten memories. In many locales, competing short lines ran parallel to one another only a short distance apart. In 1893, this period of railroad expansion in Minnesota came to a crashing halt with a great financial panic that swept the nation. By 1900, as the surviving main line railroads consolidated and swallowed up the others, much of the old short-line trackage was abandoned.

41. This was Osee Matson Hall, a prominent Red Wing attorney who had a summer home at Wacouta Point on Lake Pepin. He was Israel Garrard's attorney and a close personal friend. He would have handled the legal matters pertaining to the land deal with the railroad.
42. When U.S. Highway 61 was built in the twentieth century, it paralleled the railroad and also the old military road between Wabasha and St. Paul. Because of Israel Garrard's gift of land to the railroad, the highway between Lake City and Red Wing hugged the east side of the railroad to pass through Frontenac Station. A portion of the old military road, now called Territorial Road, survives today just to the west of the railroad.
43. Now County Road 2.
44. Columbia Street is now part of U.S. Highway 61.
45. St. John's has its roots in the German families who originally settled in Old Frontenac and Florence Township. Many descendants of the original families who arrived in Old Frontenac in the mid-nineteenth century are members of the congregation today.
46. Lake Pepin has always attracted sailors and continues to do so to the present. Hundreds of sailboats, large and small, make their summer homes at one of the three marinas presently along the lakeshore. A drive along the shore on a pleasant summer day gives a view of large numbers of sails, sharing the lake with power yachts and barge tows.
47. In addition to banking and other business interests, Lewis Garrard served two terms as mayor of Lake City and also two terms in the Minnesota state legislature.
48. The rules of their order dictated that the nuns could not enter a private residence. Thus, Israel would always entertain them on the front porch of St. Hubert's Lodge, overlooking the lake.

49. Jeptha Garrard's farm lay on the north side of McLean Avenue (today's County Road 2) as did the lands belonging to his stepbrother, Nathaniel McLean. An early aerial photo shows a view of their outbuildings across from Christ Church. When Frontenac State Park was established, the Minnesota Department of Natural Resources leveled these buildings and allowed the land to revert to nature.
50. The portion of Point No Point owned by Israel Garrard, containing the quarry, limekiln and a lumber storage facility was just north of Frontenac Point where the hotel was located. It is still called Garrard's Bluff by the local residents of Frontenac today. The area is now part of Frontenac State Park.
51. The hired operator, a professional parachutist, died a few years later in a fall from a Cincinnati skyscraper.
52. Jeptha attained some local notoriety when newspapers from St. Paul and Red Wing sent reporters to observe test flights. The resulting articles were somewhat derisive, with one referring to the unnamed pilot as "the necessary idiot." But Jeptha was not alone in his quest for man-powered flight during the 1890s. Many inventors pursued the same dream. A significant number of these so-called "ornithopters" were developed, many of far less practicality than the one created by Jeptha Garrard. In a few cases, the tests of these were filmed, and virtually everyone has seen these early clips, shown in documentaries about early manned aircraft. The clips are typically accompanied by tinkly period music and show the failures of these experiments in an almost slapstick fashion, ignoring the serious nature of the inventors. Two of these early inventors were brothers Wilbur and Orville Wright, who first experimented with manned gliders built in their bicycle shop in Dayton, Ohio. Replacing human power with a gasoline engine, they finally achieved their goal in 1903 and gave birth to a century of innovation in aircraft development.
53. I have firsthand knowledge of the unpredictability of Lake Pepin's weather. While sailing alone on an otherwise uneventful summer morning, my boat received such a gust, costing me my mast, standing rigging and both sails. While I still sail on the lake, I do so with much more alertness to weather systems in the area.
54. The nature of the storm that struck the *Sea Wing* is still unclear. Weather conditions were conducive to tornadoes, and a number of them had struck towns north of St. Paul that afternoon. A surviving crew member stated that he saw a waterspout about five hundred yards dead ahead just before the vessel was struck and capsized, but this was never fully verified. So it will never be known if the *Sea Wing* was victim of a tornado or the notorious straight-line winds that are a part of the Lake Pepin environment.

For a fuller description of the disaster, rescue operations and the resulting investigation, see *The Sea Wing Disaster* by Frederick Johnson.

55. The sight of the rugged old general and the attractive young actress riding about the village in his buggy attracted local gossip, and rumors spread of a romantic affair. Years after Israel's death, an interview with no less a source than the nun in charge at Villa Maria laid these rumors to rest. According to her, there had been absolutely no impropriety in the friendship. Miss Dressler never returned to Frontenac after her brief stay there.
56. A soldier to the last, Israel Garrard was buried in uniform, with his old battle flag. His pallbearers were Ed Hunecke, Louis Carlson, John Schennach, William Patton, Casper Carsteson and Charles Gohrke, all longtime friends and devoted employees.
57. The sale price is recorded as being $10,000.
58. A great deal of local oral history has been told and retold over the years regarding Bully Wells, Evert Westervelt and the Garrard brothers. This includes the stories of the buildings in the village. Like all oral history, the true story becomes blurred over time. Many of these stories have been accepted at face value by previous writers and thus presented me with the task of refining the facts wherever possible by resorting to original primary sources and careful reevaluation of the history. Fortunately, the result does not fall too far from the existing lore, but the careful reader may find the differences. To the many descendants of the village's original residents, my only hope is that I have done justice to their ancestors.
59. I still remember vividly my own first visit to Frontenac. Forty years ago, a less than favorable sailing day at Lake City led to a lazy exploration of the immediate area north of Lake City. Driving along the lake side on County Road 2, one is first presented with a view of Villa Maria sitting on its beautiful site. Farther along, a sharp rise up to the terrace level and the large homes of Frontenac appear as if a curtain was rising. The magic of this scene has led me back to the same site many times in the intervening years, and that first impression is still always repeated.

Introduction to the Buildings

60. A prime example of this type of educated amateur was Thomas Jefferson, who kept redesigning and modifying Monticello until his death.
61. This influence can be demonstrated by a drive through farm country in the Midwest or careful observation of buildings in the smaller communities

where urban expansion is less likely to have taken its toll. Pockets of similarity in style and use of local materials show the hand of the same builder.

62. Landscape architect Andrew Jackson Downing almost singlehandedly established the popular Gothic Revival and Italian Villa styles with the publications of *Cottage Residences* (1844) and *Rural Residences* (1837). Numbered plates showed elevations, floor plans and details for a number of houses. A large number of equivalent works were published for the Greek Revival, but the bible for most carpenters was Asher Benjamin's *The Builder's Guide* (1841). Operating an early school for architects in Boston, Benjamin popularized Greek Revival with numerous articles and plan books published between 1826 and 1844. It is interesting to note that today, more than 150 years later, plan books are still published and can be seen on every newsstand. The only major difference with their nineteenth-century ancestors is that now they are marketing stock plan sets instead of showing every aspect of the house. They are still a viable alternative to the expense of a professional architect.

63. Prior to the 1840s, homes were usually constructed using the old traditional European method of post and beam framing, requiring heavy timbers and meticulous fitting of mortises and tenons. What nails were involved were usually hand forged locally. The introduction of nail-making machinery gave rise to the availability of standardized (and relatively cheap) hardware for builders. Nails and standard-sized lumber gave rise to a new method of framing, nicknamed "balloon" due to its relative lightness and ease of erection. Based on the two-by-four stud and a standard interval of sixteen inches, it is still used today in virtually all residential construction in the United States.

64. Furniture and furnishings of the 1820s were designed in a richer "Greek" style, rejecting the more formal colonial patterns. Ladies' dresses of relaxed fit, and without the hoops and stays of before, became popular among all classes. The poetry of Lord Byron, a strong supporter of Greek independence, found a far more enthusiastic audience in America than in his home country of England. A lasting legacy of this fascination with things Greek was the many cities founded at this period and given Greek names. The first occurrences were mostly in New York (Athens, Troy, Sparta, Syracuse, etc.) and the custom spread from there, with many cities similarly named in other states.

65. The home of Willard Bunnell, just south of Winona, Minnesota, on Highway 61, was built in 1858 and is a good example of the Gothic Revival style pioneered by Andrew Jackson Downing. Downing's other advocated

style is represented in the Italianate mansion of Patrick Rahilly, a few miles east of Lake City on Wabasha County Road 15. It was not built until 1880 but is a near duplication of an 1859 mansion originally in Rochester. Another excellent example of Italianate design (but with some surprising Moorish touches) is the Huff-Lamberton House, located in Winona.

66. Probably the most notable of these is Roger Kennedy's *Historic Homes of Minnesota*, originally published in 1967 and reissued in 2006. In it, three of the terrace houses are described: St. Hubert's Lodge, Locust Lodge and Greystone.

67. The Historic American Buildings Survey (HABS) was established in 1933 by the U.S. Parks Service as a make-work relief project for unemployed architects, draftsmen and photographers. The database created is an invaluable asset for historic preservationists and led to the creation of two sister organizations by the Park Service. In 1969, Historic American Engineering Record (HAER) was put in place to document significant engineering projects. In 2000, the Historic American Landscape Survey (HALS) was added. All of these projects provide seasonal employment for students, and the results are available online via the U.S. Park Services website.

THE TERRACE AREA

68. Currently, there is one exception. The owners of St. Hubert's Lodge have made a determined assault on the growth facing them on the brow of the terrace. For the time being, that house has its views restored and can be seen from the lake.

69. These features may not be part of the original structure and were most likely added in about 1900, when the rear addition was built.

70. Local lore states that Israel Garrard was out hunting for small game while the house was being built and encountered a magnificent buck deer. Because of the beauty of the animal, Israel opted not to take the easy shot and let it depart. The incident reminded him of the legend of St. Hubert, who spared a stag when he saw the sign of the cross between its antlers, and he named his home accordingly.

71. Israel probably had seen similar houses along the river north of its confluence with the Ohio. Examples of this style still exist in St. Louis, Galena, Prairie du Chien and elsewhere.

72. No reason for this is recorded. Local legend says it was because Israel was so short that he saw no need for the added height of his rooms. Photos of

Israel show him to be of slightly less than average height, but not so short as to cause him to have a complex about it.

73. The Garrards' hospitality seemed boundless. Before the hotel was established, a number of long-term guests occupied space in one of the houses overlooking the lake. One was author Charles King, who wrote an entire novel while occupying an upstairs bedroom at St. Hubert's Lodge. Another was artist Augustus Moore, who came in 1862 and spent a full year with Lewis and Florence at Dacotah Cottage.

74. The house was maintained by a series of local men hired for the purpose. By the 1920s, the current caretaker had pretty much claimed the property for his own use, storing unused farm tools and equipment in the parlors and raising pigs in the large side yard.

75. This was the son of Osee Matson Hall, the Red Wing attorney who had partnered with Israel Garrard in the negotiations with the railroad in 1872. George Garrard supposedly sold Dacotah Cottage to Hall's son in appreciation of their respective fathers' longtime friendship.

76. The son of the family, Ted Hall, many years later published his personal memoir, *Growing with the Grass,* documenting what it was like to grow up in Frontenac in the 1930s. Details are given regarding the reclamation and refurbishing of Dacotah Cottage, and a number of anecdotes describe everyday life in the village. See bibliography for details.

77. Fowler was also a phrenologist and an advocate of free love. He had three wives in all and fathered many children, some of them when in his seventies.

78. Concrete as a building material was nothing new. Used by the Romans in their most ambitious projects, it remains common up to the present day. Many of the great stone cathedrals of Europe are of concrete construction, poured between two narrow, laid-up stone walls and reinforced with lengths of iron chain sunk in it. By the 1850s, it was known by a number of other names: grout, gravel wall, "pebble dash" or just plain cement. All of these are synonymous with "concrete," the term I use for consistency.

79. The first documented builder of octagonal barns was a German builder named Clausen in Ozaukee County, Wisconsin. He found that the octagonal shape better resisted the high winds coming from Lake Michigan. Further benefits derived from the lack of interior columns or bearing walls, allowing free passage of equipment and supplies. The concept grew, and today Wisconsin and Minnesota have many eight-sided barns scattered around the countryside.

80. Minnesota has a number of examples of octagonal houses, mostly built in wood. Poured concrete houses of non-octagonal shape are rarer. To locate

these, the reader is referred to Roger Kennedy's *Historic Homes of Minnesota* and to *The National Register of Historic Places in Minnesota*, compiled by Mary Ann Nord. See the bibliography for details.

81. Each of the terrace houses would have had one of these icehouses. The poured concrete afforded excellent insulation from the summer heat and preserved a supply of ice harvested from the lake. Only two icehouses survive, one at Greystone and another at Winona Cottage.
82. This legend of the suicidal maiden is a popular one along the upper Mississippi River, it seems. The city of Winona to the south is named for the same princess who supposedly jumped from its prominent landmark bluff, Sugar Loaf. Other examples of the same story exist wherever some steep cliff is near the river. The lovelorn girl(s) of this legend join the fictitious warrior Hiawatha as icons of the lore that derived from the romanticism of early settlers in the region, eventually finding their way into the poetry of Longfellow and others.
83. Except for corner and gate posts, the entire wall was constructed without mortar, using rough ashlar stones from the nearby quarry.
84. When the Chicago and Northwestern Railroad built north from Chicago into Wisconsin in the mid-1800s, it skirted the western shore of Lake Geneva. This easy access to the city caused the creation of Fontana, which quickly became an exclusive enclave of summer homes for some of Chicago's most prominent families. A visit to Fontana today yields a feast of well-preserved Victorian-era "cottages," both great and small.

Frontenac Point

85. In Ted Hall's personal memoir, *Growing with the Grass*, he recounts the time in the early 1930s when Drs. William and Charles Mayo arrived for dinner aboard Dr. Will's large yacht, the *Northstar*. A group of local boys swimming near the landing approached the brothers and asked permission to dive from the top of the high pilot house. After a brief consultation, it was granted.
86. The LeDuc Mansion upriver in Hastings, Minnesota, has a fully preserved icehouse dating from the period. I used it to draw conclusions and inferences to describe the structure at Frontenac.
87. The original site of the Kittle House, before it was moved to the point in 1881, was at the northeast corner of Wood Avenue and Sumner Street.

THE VILLAGE

88. In the Dakota language, this is translated as: "They say it is sacred."
89. Local lore states that the school originally occupied land in the middle of the village and was later moved to its current site to place it closer to Frontenac Station sometime after the railroad came through. Research into abstracts and old school records shows no data to support this story. The current site is most probably the original location.
90. Just prior to the closing of the school, *Life* magazine did a feature on one-room schools. Frontenac School was chosen as a typical example, and a photo of it, with a group of students playing in the schoolyard, appeared in the article.
91. Another story is that during a renovation of the house in the 1980s, a small girl at the scene mispronounced the name "Hunecke" as "Honeybee," and the current owner adopted the nickname.
92. Chicken dinners at the hotel, especially on summer Sundays, were popular with locals and tourists alike. Through the life of the hotel, up until its closing in 1939, countless chickens from the Hunecke coops were consumed. An interesting advertisement for the Frontenac Inn, which ran in a local newspaper in 1935, gave the price of a chicken dinner as thirty-five cents. A full day's lodging, including room and board, was only $2.50.
93. This was Garrard Beck, whose mother was Evelyn Garrard Beck. A frequent visitor to Frontenac, Mr. Beck ultimately changed his name to Israel Garrard Beck to honor his great-grandfather.
94. An example of Florence Strupe's activism occurred in 1995, when Northern States Power proposed a facility in Florence Township, near Frontenac Station, to store radioactive waste from its nuclear plant on Prairie Island. Local forces mustered and managed to defeat the proposal, enlisting support at the state government level and also in the media. An article in the *Minneapolis Star Tribune*, dated April 30, 1995, has a photo of Florence, then ninety-four, at the gate of Little Dacotah. In the accompanying interview, she concisely and articulately pleaded the case against the project and its impact on Florence Township.
95. Will Lubeck's talent for carpentry was obviously a family trait. In a letter to Israel Garrard, written during the 1862 remodel of Dacotah Cottage, Lewis Garrard writes: "Hunecke, Lubeck and the others seem to be unable to work without a great deal of joking and shouting." But then he goes on to express his confidence in their skill and craftsmanship and his new bride's pleasure in the results.

Churches

96. Richard Upjohn was a busy and successful architect, known in particular for his large church projects in the East. A native of England, he arrived in America in 1829 to begin a career spanning more than four decades. He designed many notable churches, one of which is Trinity Church at the end of Wall Street in New York City. Preferring stone as a material in his larger projects, he also saw the emergence of the vertical board and batten method of construction in the Gothic-style residences then gaining popularity. He embraced this style and created a large number of small wooden churches across the northeastern states. The requests for plans were overwhelming, leading to the publication of *Rural Architecture* and freeing him up to concentrate on his larger projects.
97. When waves of immigrants from the northern European countries flooded into the Midwestern United States in the 1840s, many were Lutheran. Used to hearing the liturgy in their own language, settlers tended to build churches along national lines. A number of Lutheran synods formed in the United States to support these various nationally oriented congregations and to provide them with clergy. St. John's is part of the Wisconsin Evangelical Lutheran Synod (WELS), historically German. The church in Frontenac was probably associated with the Evangelical Lutheran Church of America (ELCA), supporting the liturgy from Norway, Denmark and Sweden.

The Long Point Area

98. When a more permanent structure was called for, the "Poteaux sur sole" method was used. This required a stone foundation with a sill of squared timber. The vertical logs of the walls were tied together at the top with a timber rafter system. This style of house prevailed everywhere the French built settlements in Missouri, Illinois and Wisconsin. The traditional American log cabin, with its horizontal notched logs, was brought much later to the frontier and was primarily the invention of immigrants from Scandinavia.
99. No actual trace of this site has been found. That it existed near the beach was documented in official reports to the governor general. Long Point is now part of Frontenac State Park, and a hiking trail leads from the parking area along County Road 2 to the beach area.

100. The site of the second and third forts is not completely known, though historians agree that it was near the site of the current Villa Maria. A careful survey of the terrain yields a best guess that it was probably situated on the knoll just to the left of the villa entrance and close to County Road 2.
101. To more fully understand nineteenth-century milling operations, visit a historic mill still in operation. This is at Pickwick, a few miles south of Winona, Minnesota. It features a large overshot wheel and millpond with dam. It is open to tours.
102. The mill site is adjacent to one of the hiking trails in Frontenac State Park. The trailhead is just off Highway 61 along County Road 2. After crossing the county road, the mill site is only a short distance along the trail, on the right. Wells creek has changed its course many times over the years and no longer runs near the site.
103. It is not surprising that a St. Louis architect was chosen. The Ursuline Order had its headquarters in that city, and still does.
104. One of these visits had sad consequences. While Israel was talking with Henry Hunecke, his favorite dog fell through an opening in the floor and was killed. Israel buried the dog in the yard of St. Hubert's Lodge and marked its grave with a small stone inscribed: "Faithful Wappie."
105. For a highly detailed account of the ceremonies, see the *Lake City Graphic* of September 8, 1891.

FRONTENAC STATION

106. Major junctions were at LaCrosse, Winona and Red Wing. Larger depots were required to accommodate transferring passengers and storage of freight.
107. George Washington Van Dusen came to Minnesota in 1862 and settled in Rochester. He became a major buyer of grain, erecting a series of elevators along the newly constructed Winona and St. Peter Railroad. He expanded his empire to include the other area railroads and moved to Minneapolis in the 1870s, when he built a major fortune as part of the burgeoning milling industry. After his death, he was returned to Rochester and buried in Oakwood Cemetery.

Bibliography

Carley, Kenneth. *The Dakota War of 1862*. St. Paul: Minnesota Historical Society Press, 1976.

Clemens, Samuel L. *Life on the Mississippi*. New York: Houghton & Company, 1874.

des Cognets, Anna Russell. *Governor Garrard of Kentucky, His Descendants & Relatives*. Edited by Louis des Cognets Jr. Princeton, NJ: 1962.

Densmore, Frances. "The Garrard Family in Frontenac." *Minnesota History Quarterly* 14 (1933).

Drury, George H. *The Historical Guide to North American Railroads*. Waukesha, WI: Kalmbach Publishing, 2000.

Fleming, J., H. Honour and N. Pevsner. The Penguin Dictionary of Architecture. London: Penguin Books, 1991.

Folwell, William Watts. *A History of Minnesota*. Vol. 1. St. Paul: Minnesota Historical Society, 1930.

Foster, Gerald. *American Houses: A Field Guide to the Architecture of the Home*. New York: Houghton Mifflin, 2004.

Garrard, Lewis H. *Wah-To-Yah and the Taos Trail, or Prairie Travel and Scalp Dances*. Cincinnati, OH: 1850.

Gebhard, David, and Tom Martinson. *A Guide to the Architecture of Minnesota*. Minneapolis: University of Minnesota Press, 1977.

Hall, Ted. *Growing with the Grass*. Ranier, MN: Rainy Lake Printing House, 1992.

Hamlin, Talbot. *Greek Revival Architecture in America*. London: Oxford University Press, 1944.

Johnson, Frederick L. *The* Sea Wing *Disaster*. Red Wing, MN: Goodhue County Historical Society, 1990.

Kennedy, Roger G. *Historic Homes of Minnesota*. St. Paul: Minnesota Historical Society Press, 2006.

Kubista, Ivan. *This Quiet Dust: A Chronicle of Old Frontenac*. Frontenac, MN: Old Frontenac Heritage Preservation Commission, 1978.

League of Women Voters of Minnesota. *Indians in Minnesota*. St. Paul, MN: 1974.

McAlester, Virginia, and Lee McAlester. *A Field Guide to American Houses*. New York: Alfred A. Knopf, 2006.

"The Mendota-Wabasha Road." In Minnesota Historic Site Pamphlet Series #10, *Tracing Minnesota's Old Government Roads*. St. Paul: Minnesota Historical Society, 1974.

Millikan, William. "The Great Treasure of the Fort Snelling Prison Camp." *Minnesota History* 62, no. 1 (Spring 2010).

Morgan, William. *The Abrams Guide to American House Styles*. New York: Abrams, 2004.

Pierson, William H. *American Buildings and Their Architects*. New York: Doubleday & Company, 1978.

Randall, J.G., and David Donald. *The Civil War and Reconstruction*. Boston: D.C. Heath & Company, 1961.

Webster, Margaret, ed. *Letters from Lewis Garrard to Sara Bella McLean* (September 1854). Webster family collection.

Yenne, Bill. *Atlas of North American Railroads*. St. Paul, MN: MBI Publishing, 2005.

Photo Credits

Cited images in this book are from the following sources:

Friends of Old Frontenac. Collected by William Webster, Frontenac, Minnesota. (Cited as "Friends Collection.")

William Flies, Frontenac, Minnesota. (Cited as "Flies Collection.")

Goodhue County Historical Society, Red Wing, Minnesota. (Cited as "GCHS.")

About the Author

Ken Allsen has had a life-long love affair with architecture and its history. He resides in Rochester, Minnesota, with his wife, Nancy.

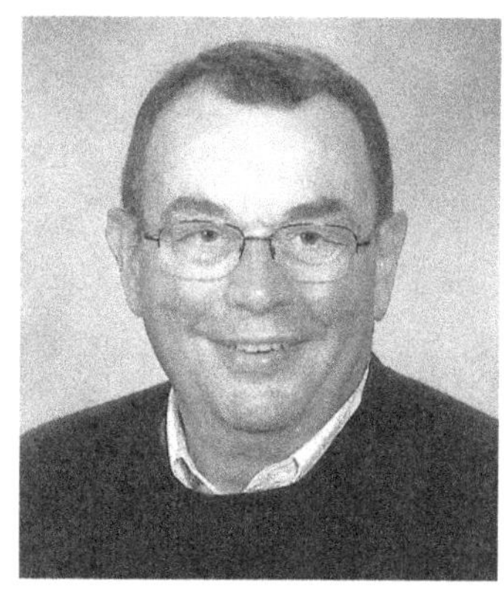

www.ingramcontent.com/pod-product-compliance
Lightning Source LLC
LaVergne TN
LVHW052342100826
845147LV00021B/1155

* 9 7 8 1 5 9 6 2 9 5 0 7 0 *